T0171407

...AND THEN SOME

Thirty-six new stories from the author of
Memoirs of a Little Italian Boy

David A. Govoni

iUniverse, Inc.
Bloomington

...AND THEN SOME

Thirty-six new stories from the author of *Memoirs of a Little Italian Boy*

iUniverse books may be ordered through booksellers or by contacting:

iUniverse
1663 Liberty Drive
Bloomington, IN 47403
www.iuniverse.com
1-800-Authors (1-800-288-4677)

ISBN: 978-1-4502-7520-0 (pbk)
ISBN: 978-1-4502-7521-7 (ebk)

Printed in the United States of America

iUniverse rev. date: 12/10/2010

Preface

The reason I wrote this book, sequel to *Memoirs of a Little Italian Boy,* is because I ended that one too abruptly. In my haste to finish the book I did forget a few things that I have since had time to remember.

My wife, Nancy, has continued to encourage me to write about everything that came to my mind. Some new story ideas have emerged from that.

So I did more writing and suddenly, here it is, a finished manuscript, and the title of it is exactly what you are reading: *...And Then Some,,* by LIB (Little Italian Boy).

Other people have also been extremely supportive when I've told them about my new book. I want to continue writing, so I hope you enjoy reading my stories as much as I do writing them.

David A. Govoni, the "Little Italian Boy"

P.S. For more information and to see what I've been up to lately, visit:

www.littleitalianboy.com.

Contents

SECTION ONE:
LOOKING BACK

Book Signing

My first book signing at *Books-A-Million* was in August, 2002. It was the first time I had done anything like this and I really didn't know what to expect. I was completely surprised by the people from our fly-in community who came to wish me well. I guess from now on, my life will be an open book for anyone to read, and I'll have to continue to behave myself.

My book had been published for several months and I needed help to be able to continue writing. The newly-formed Florida Writers Association met for the first time in November, 2003 in Orlando. I became a member at this convention and their purpose was writers helping writers. We chose classes that we wanted to attend depending on the type of material that would most benefit each of us.

Professional writers conducted the classes, during which valuable information helped many of us understand how important it is to have proper wording and a good knowledge of the English language. I had no idea how little I knew about phraseology: I listened intently to the many tips about writing, and then I wondered how I could have possibly written *Memoirs of a Little Italian Boy*. Many thanks to Kris, my proofreader, who should get a gold star.

When I first started writing, I had no idea what I was doing. I just kept on banging away at the keys, like I'm doing now. But at the conference, after one of the workshops, I was packing my books and notes into my briefcase when a young lady came up to me and told me how much I had inspired her. She bought my book to give to her dad and asked me to sign it to him. She told me that her dad was 80 years old and had been in WWII, and that she had been trying to get him to write about his experiences. After she read what I had written, she threw her arms around me because she knew that my book would inspire him to write. She gave me a hug and a kiss, and went off with tears in her eyes. Wow, that gave me a huge responsibility, which is a reason for writing well.

There were other writers selling their books at the convention, but I felt I was the only one having any luck because I sold all but two copies out of the 25 I had brought. As people walked by, when anyone looked in my direction or showed any interest, I announced, "I am the Little Italian Boy." When they heard me say that and stopped to look at the cover of my book, it gave me a chance to tell them more of what was in it. Most people showed interest in what I had to say and walked off with either a signed book or at least a smile on their face. I love talking to people and I guess it shows by the number of sales I made. I tell everyone that if I had known I was going to have this much fun I would have started writing 40 years ago.

While I was writing this, the doorbell rang. A young, Fed Ex lady dressed in tight shorts and a tight, flowered blouse was delivering a package at the front door. I had to sign for it and while I was writing my name on her computer notepad, I asked if she liked to read. I told her about an exciting new book out: *Memoirs of a Little Italian Boy.* She smiled and asked if it was my book. It's funny she knew right away that it was. Is that possible? Well anyway, she said she would buy one and as she walked away I jokingly said, "It has nothing in it about my sex life."

She stopped, turned and with a quizzical look on her face said, "When are you going to write about that?"

I laughed and told her that I hadn't made any plans to write it because the book would be so thick it would probably have to sell for $50. I came back in the house chuckling to myself, knowing that I would never write about my sex life!

A month later, at another book signing at *Books-A-Million*, a long-time friend showed up. He stood in front of me and said casually, "I'm Earl Mugridge." I was speechless because it had been 50 years since I had last seen him. We had worked together at the Beverly Airport in Massachusetts. After the bombing of Pearl Harbor all airports along each coast of the U.S. were closed for security. Earl and I, just the two of us, were given the job of helping move the whole operation of airplanes and anchor rope tie-downs.

Our company was moved 100 miles inland, away from the coast to Claremont, New Hampshire. During that time we spent about ten days preparing for the training planes to arrive. Earl and I bunked in what was later used as an office, and I can still hear him say, "Rise and Shine" first thing every morning. Now, a half a century later, here we were: We talked for a short time about the past and then made plans to meet at a later date.

At the same book signing, two little ladies stood quietly, waiting for me to finish signing my last few books. One walked up and told me her name was Laura Govoni. She had seen an article in *The News-Journal* about this book signing, noticed that our names were spelled the same, and come to see me. She said her father had been born in Bologna, Italy, and had landed in Boston when he came to this country. I told her that my father was also born in Bologna, Italy, and had landed in Boston at the beginning of the century: What a surprise it was for both of us. She agreed to come to dinner one day in the future so that we could talk and find out if we were related. She bought a book and said she would read it very carefully. I was really looking forward to meeting with her again.

Several weeks went by before we met Laura Govoni and her friend Jan, to start what would blossom into a close relationship. We talked with them over dinner one evening and found that Laura had hand written a whole book on pharmacology. She and Jan are both doctors of pharmacology and the book has been in use for many years. At this writing Laura admitted to being 92 years of age, and Jan was 87. They both are amazingly intelligent ladies and quite agile and can walk anywhere we do and almost as fast. We have gone as far as we know how to check our common heritage, but seem to end up nowhere. We just say we are very close cousins because that's we want to be. The one thing about all of this is that I never realized there were so many women who are married to Italians, or who have Italians somewhere in the family.

One day I stood in line at the post office and when I handed the postal clerk a package, I told her that it was my book and I was sending it to a friend. She was thrilled that she was talking to a real-live author and congratulated me on such an accomplishment. I told her that it was a story about my life and she said that I should send it to Oprah, which may not be a bad idea.

One lady said that she had read my book and asked if anyone knew the name of the plant that I called "frog belly." In the book, I described how I got blood poisoning from a cut on my thumb and how, although the doctor lanced it to make it bleed, it continued to hurt and would not heal. I explained how my mother had talen a leaf from the plant, squashed it and bandaged it to my thumb. Overnight it drew out all the poison, the pain went away and my thumb healed up. The green leaf that she took from the dome plant had a thickness to it and when she squeezed the leaf it brought liquid to the surface. This is what my mom wrapped around my finger, with a bandage to hold it on. When she took the bandage off the next day, a soft clump of matter was hanging out of the cut. She took a pair of tweezers and pulled it out of my thumb and my thumb healed up almost immediately.

All who have read my book find different things in it to talk about. According to them, there is a wealth of information in it. Many of the older generation, who came here from the old country, started in the fruit business because they knew nothing else. Some were blacksmiths, some were orchid grape farmers or wine makers and most all were singers because they are happy people, just like I am.

To this day I have not found the scientific name for that miraculous plant and, since my mother is no longer with us, perhaps I never will.

Ouch!

Writing about my early life in *Memoirs of a Little Italian Boy* put me in touch with my childhood: I'm still dredging up memories that exist on the back burner of my brain. I have been reminded by my diligent readers that I could not have covered every aspect of my life. I couldn't imagine what they were talking about but in reminiscing, I may have left out a few details that I didn't think were important then, but I do now. Here are some examples:

My mother could take a lot of pain and to this day I don't know how she did. Once the family had gone for a ride in our new 1927 Buick 7-passenger sedan. It was easy to tell that a bunch of us went, because there were exactly 10 of us in this 7 passenger car. Pa was driving, kind of getting instructions from brothers Francis, Henry, Joseph and Douglas, while I and my sisters, Ida, and Rita, were sitting in the fold-down seats in the middle row of the car and Ma, with a neighbor Maria, were sitting all the way in the back seat.

When we pulled into our yard after a nice long ride in the country, there was no set procedure for disembarking, which means getting out of the car. We bailed out of that brand new vehicle with excitement and the thrill of having been on the road in such a modern and luxurious automobile of the time. It now reminds me of how a Boeing 767 pulls into the terminal and comes to a full stop, and everyone gets up. Our whole family got up and bailed out, except for Pa, who was wiping his brow after having an intense driving lesson, and Ma who was still sitting in the back seat, talking to her Italian friend, before she realized everyone was getting out.

It may have been lucky for her that car door hinges were not precision made, with close tolerances, as they are today. The fact is that the rear doors in those old cars were called suicide doors because they were hinged in the rear and swung open towards the front of the car. These kinds of doors were very dangerous, especially if the door opened while the car was moving ahead.

Ma placed her fingers in the wide hinge part of the door jam to pull herself ahead so that she could get out, too. Someone ahead of her jumped out and slammed the rear door shut, forgetting she was behind him. At the same moment, he realized his mistake and opened the door because he saw the excruciating pain on Ma's face and knew he had caught her fingers in the doorjamb. She didn't even cry out or say anything because she was breathless. She just held her hand in her lap, with her eyes closed, and I'm sure she prayed that her hand wasn't completely smashed. If you could have seen the look on her face, as I did, you would have cried. Luckily she had no broken bones but had slightly crushed fingers that were swollen and ached for days.

Not wanting to seem like a sissy, I always tried not to show the amount of suffering I was going through. Take the time when I pretended to smoke—of all things—a real, live firecracker. I was with a few kids from my neighborhood. Most were older, and I was acting foolish like them, pretending to smoke a cigar. The only difference was, they were picking up blown-up fire crackers which we called "salutes." These were about the size of a small cigar. I was the smart one because I had found a new salute that was in perfect condition. I stuck it in my mouth without thinking, I lit it, and it went off. I thought I had blown my head off; the inside of my mouth felt like it was full of sand and I was, momentarily, completely deaf from the sound of the explosion When that thing went off in my mouth I can't even describe how it really felt without saying some bad words.

I do remember being badly burned inside my mouth and face. Why it didn't kill me, I'll never know. I have no recollection of my recovery or of how long it took: I must have been in shock.

I don't have to tell you how much it hurt getting my front teeth knocked in at age 12 when I fell on my face onto a concrete wall, walking home from the movies on a Saturday afternoon. My neighbor Albert, who was walking alongside me, kept bumping into my elbows. In an effort to move away from him I put my left foot too close to the wall and was not able to get my right foot through the space. The jacket I was wearing was too small and I had my hands jammed into the side pockets tightly and was not able to get them out in time to stop my fall.

Another time, I busted my nose sliding with my brother Doug on the back of his sled after he decided to steer under a wooden sawhorse, instead of around it. It had been put there, with a lantern hanging on each end, to barricade cars from coming down the end of the street. I took a direct hit to my nose with the two by four, the horizontal part that holds the four legs strongly together, and this all happened at the bottom of Prospect Hill. Every time I got hurt, I bled profusely and I still do, especially when I get nosebleeds.

The only time that I deserved to be hurt was when I got hit by a car backing out of a Plymouth dealer in Salem. Saturday afternoons we were allowed to bring our own cars into the garage and work on them until 5 p.m. Then we had to stop work and get our cars out of the garage to make room for the brand new cars that were on display across the street. One of the men had finished working on his automobile and was backing it out of the garage at a high rate of speed. When I stepped into the path of this speeding car and got hit, I went sailing through the air. All sorts of things went through my mind, like, *how does anyone think of what is going to happen when he is about to hit the concrete floor after flying through the air?* Looking back, it does seem incredible that I had time to think, because my mind went into shock overdrive. I was so completely relaxed which I think saved me from being really hurt badly. I thought, *I've just been hit by a blue car because it spun my head around and I saw the blue paint on the trunk of the car.* I must have traveled ten or twelve feet through the air and was not scratched or bleeding.

One time at my hangar I was pulling my plane out through the big sliding doors. For some reason, the clearance on the left wing was very close, and I was afraid of hitting a truck that was parked in the way. In order for the wing tip to clear the truck, I had to move the nose wheel back and forth as I was pulling it. I accidentally let the rod that goes through the wheel slip out of place while I was pulling hard on the tow bar and when it did, I fell backwards.

When I think of it now, time really changed gears because of the many things that have happened to me. When taking home movies, by changing the settings on a camera, you can take more frames per second and make the picture appear to be in slow motion. That's what it seemed like to me, when I was falling backward with nothing to stop me: Time went into slow motion. I was relaxed and remembered to stay bent, so that my behind hit first, then my shoulders, but the impact was so hard that my head hit the concrete with the strangest sound I ever heard, and believe me I heard it. The man who was standing in the next hangar heard it, too.

He rushed over to me and for a few seconds I lay there: I didn't want to get up. I wanted to be sure that I could get up and stand without assistance. I started to laugh and wonder how it had happened.

For a moment I thought that the tow bar had broken but after examining it, I saw it was my fault because I let it slip out of the wheel. My head never really hurt, I did not get a headache from it, and the bump on my head didn't knock any more sense into me than I had before.

Business Beginnings

In 1936, when I was ten years old, I started working on a regular basis in my family's grocery store in Beverly, MA. It was during the summer months when I was on school vacation. I had just started in the sixth grade at Briscoe Junior High, a completely different and grown-up school. The school day ended at 2:00 p.m. and I went to work at the store from 2:30 until 6:00 p.m. every day. On Saturdays I worked from 9:00 until 6:00, and during summer vacation I worked full days. By age 12, during school days I worked every other night from 6:00 until 11:00. On these nights I had the afternoons off.

Working those crazy hours didn't seem to bother me then because I was young and full of energy, but as I grew older it took its toll, and my off hours were spent napping although I still had no trouble sleeping at night. I couldn't understand why, when I tried to do my homework, I would fall asleep and it wasn't until recently that I realized the answer. It finally dawned on me that I was so tired from working those long hours that I fell asleep while trying to read and do my homework assignments. I guess I was lucky to get through school with passing grades.

In those days there were no self-service grocery stores so we, the workers, did all the fetching. When I finished with a customer's list, I marked the price of each item on a big brown paper bag with a pencil which was usually stuck behind my ear, and I added the columns quickly and accurately. I didn't know how to make change but watched my brothers and learned everything from them. My weekly pay was fifty cents and sometimes I had to ask for it when my older brothers conveniently forgot to pay me. By the age of twelve I was fully capable taking care of customers and often handled the store myself. When it was really busy and I had to take care of three or more customers at one time, I could to call for help. The house where we lived was right in back of the store and there was generally someone who could come to my rescue.

My brother Doug, who was seven years older than I, left his job with Walter Baker's Chocolate factory in Boston to come back to my Dad's store and take charge in the early thirties. This was during the depression when business was bad everywhere. I became Doug's right-hand man. He was a man with vision and we worked well together. Little by little, new ideas started taking shape in the form of a more streamlined store.

Business got better and then the store became too small and Doug decided to knock down the wall to the adjacent store, which was owned by my dad. It was quite an undertaking but very exciting because for me, this was progress: We were going places. When that was finally done, shelves were made for the new addition; then we had two doors to enter and exit the store.

Keeping vegetables cool and fresh was always a problem until Doug found a company that sold a modern vegetable display case. It was hooked up to water and had four pipes sticking up, with small, misty sprayers to sprinkle the lettuce and other veggies that needed to be kept moist. Of course when my father saw that new piece of equipment coming into the store he raised his eyebrow and said, *"Povrita America."* I didn't quite understand the phrase but took it to mean we would all be in the poor house if it didn't work. Well, it did work just fine and it took a lot of courage for Doug to do some of the things he did because he always had to answer to Pa if it didn't.

The front display windows were always kept clean and sparkling so people could see in, and new displays were added to catch their eyes. Then one night Doug and I were standing in the store, looking out the front windows, when all of a sudden he said that we had to brighten up the looks of the store so it could be seen by everyone driving up Elliot Street. He made plans to put up a ceiling made of the new stuff just out, called acoustical tile, and to get rid of the old-fashioned lights with globes that hung from the ceilings. Then, new fluorescent lights were put up in a straight line in the front and in the back with connecting lights at the ends, forming a long rectangle. With 26 units in all, each with two lamps, when the switch was turned on for the first time we knew how Thomas Edison must have felt when he lit up the town with his new electric light bulbs.

It was the talk of the town because suddenly there was light, just like in the Bible. I'm sure that some of the birds flying south thought that we went to a lot of trouble to light a beacon to help them on their journey. It helped business, and sales started to grow beyond our expectations.

I graduated high school in June of 1941, got married, and continued working in the store until July, when I got a job at Beverly Airport as apprentice mechanic. Then on December 7th the Japanese bombed Pearl Harbor and the government closed all the coastal airports. I was hired to help move the operations to Clermont, NH. The following December, I enlisted in the Navy and served there until April, 1946.

After my discharge, I went back to work at the store, doing things that had been neglected during the war, such as painting everything outside the house which was now a part of the store. When the painting was done Doug bought a brand new ice cream machine and put it in the store's front window. He put me in charge of the whole operation, which kept me running. I learned how to make the ice cream but then I had to carry the big empty containers all the way through the house and down the cellar stairs, to wash them in scalding hot water and disinfect and dry them. Then I carried them back up the stairs to make them ready to be filled with ice cream again. This went on all through the summer months and business was developing rapidly. I dipped and scooped ice cream and washed containers and carried them up and down stairs until one afternoon I became ill. My work was done at 4:30 p.m. and although I was supposed to stay until 6:00, I figured I would go home to Topsfield and go to bed to keep from getting really sick. Because my brother Doug, who was in charge that day, was nowhere to be found, I asked a fellow employee to tell Doug I had gone home early because I was sick. Doug overreacted and we had words. I decided it was time to strike out on my own.

After I recovered from what was actually pneumonia, I went into business going from house to house with fruit and veggies, then I bought a little meat market and grocery store in Topsfield. In May of the following year, a man came along and made me an offer on the store. I took advantage of the opportunity to escape the dreadful winter, pulled up stakes, and my wife and I moved to Miami, Florida in April of 1950.

I can't tell you much about the rebuilding of Pa's store because I was in Florida. My understanding was that Doug built new concrete walls around the house, then tore down the house where I was born, the house with all the memories of my childhood, the notches that I cut in the doorjamb as I grew taller, the banister I slid down, the bedroom where I slept with all my brothers growing up, the parlor with the piano I wished I could play.

Without my help, Doug continued to tear down walls and expand the store, but I had literally left my mark. With every partition that was torn down, to make way for the new supermarket, they found pieces of wood with my name, the date and the time. I wrote on these pieces of wood and threw them into the partitions as the original house and store walls were being expanded in the hope that someday, someone would find them and remember that the Little Italian Boy had once poured heart and soul into that business.

Oops!

During the many years I worked for Eastern Airlines in Miami, a lot of things happened. Some were good and some were bad, some were funny and some were sad. You can fit this story into one of those categories, and you can be the judge.

While at Eastern, I was driving a company motor scooter because I had to pick up parts from another location on the base in Miami. The distance from one building to another is quite far as you can imagine. Jets need a lot of space to move around. They are big, and it's not uncommon to be inside a building on the first or second floor, near a window, and see one of our big jet planes as it slowly taxis by, or is towed by a tractor. It is a never-ending show that seems to hypnotize me with its sheer immensity.

On this particular day another mechanic and I had several heavy parts to pick up. The scooter had a box-like container in the front, which has one wheel in the rear and two in the front. It is designed to seat two mechanics and their tools as they drive to different locations on the base. I was driving, and he was sitting on a seat in the box. As we were coming around the end of a building we came upon a big platform truck. It was parked next to another truck that had a lifting device, like a boom you might see on an auto wrecker only much bigger.

Two men were preparing to lift a big, metal, box-like container off the back of a platform truck with lifting cables that were being attached. I stopped the scooter and walked towards a man who looked like he was in charge and asked what the object was. The object on the truck was a new hydraulic test stand we were expecting for our shop. It was big and heavy, about twice the size of an old upright piano, and had a bunch of dials on the front and metal panels and pipes sticking out of it.

The four men attached a separate cable to each corner and then to one larger, main cable ring that hung over the middle. They lifted the cabinet very slowly, and stopped about three inches above the platform of the truck. Then the idea was to drive the truck out from under the cabinet. For some reason or other the top cable didn't look strong enough to me and I told the one man in charge that he should use a stronger top cable, but he assured me it would hold and yelled at the truck driver to pull ahead, slowly, out from under the cabinet.

I stepped out of the way when he started the truck's engine. Just as he drove the truck a little more than halfway out from under the cabinet, the cable snapped. Down came the cabinet, half on and half off the truck, which made the cabinet turn on its side and then crash land onto the ground with a bone wrenching crunch. It had dropped six feet onto one corner and twisted everything out of shape. There it lay in a heap of twisted junk, totally destroyed, and it had to be sent back to the manufacturer. Later I heard that a new unit replaced this one because it was specially designed for Eastern Airlines.

The noise attracted a crowd of Saturday afternoon quarterbacks, including some of the big bosses, so I figured it was time to leave and let them find out what happened. I'm glad no one was hurt but that was one time that someone should have listened to the Little Italian Boy.

Making Things Easier At Eastern

During my years at Eastern Airlines, I occasionally worked inside the cabins of the Lockheed Constellations, fixing passenger seats that were broken or needed adjustment. The aircraft came into the bay, as it is called: A bay is part of a long building, with an overhanging roof that covers the front half of each aircraft. Five aircraft can be parked side-by-side on the north side of the building. The same number can be parked on the south side, nose-to-nose with the ones on the north side. The bays make it possible for crews to work three shifts during inclement weather, and have their aircraft ready to fly in the morning.

One day Captain Eddie Rickenbacker, the head of Eastern at that time, happened to come on board one of the company planes to look at some new equipment in the cockpit. He walked past me and five other mechanics who were working nearby. He spoke to us as if he knew each of us personally, saying, "Hello, men, how is everything going today?" He was a personable man and would stop to talk or answer any question asked of him by anybody.

I wrote him several letters regarding conditions on some airplanes that I thought needed immediate attention. Naturally, I tried to go through normal channels but was unable to, for one reason or another, which led me to write letters instead. He either answered my letters promptly or directed them to the proper department.

One time I wanted to get in touch with one of the vice-presidents in the company, but was unable to get through to him. I had given up trying to convince my immediate supervisors, so I called another V.P. I kept calling but he was always unavailable, in a meeting or out of town. I called so much that he must have contacted my general foreman and told him to bring me to his office. You know, it's pretty damn bad when an employee has to take such drastic measures to be heard.

Well anyway, my general foreman came storming down the stairs from his office on the third floor and all but took me by the nape of the neck and said, "Stop what you're doing and drive me across to the 1011 hangar." He didn't say another word to me about where we were going or why.

We went charging up the stairs into a big office with a desk about a mile long. We sat there about five minutes and in walked Vice-President Hall. His first words were not very friendly: "What is it you wanted to talk to me about?"

I started by saying that I worked in the airstair department and when a Boeing 727 came into one of our many stations with an airstair that did not work, maintenance had to drive a specially designed stair truck to the plane to unload passengers. Then maintenance had to call us in Miami to deliver a new set of stairs to wherever that plane was due to land later, where they would have people who could make the change. We always had a spare set of stairs in a steel container just waiting for this kind of situation.

One evening a stock man came to my department and was looking for a stair unit that was ready to be shipped and an empty container to go with it. I asked him why he needed the empty container. He said that they always shipped an empty container to have something to put the inoperative stair into when it was removed from the plane. Then they installed the good stair into the plane and sent both containers back to Miami, one full and one empty. A container weighed 500 pounds and the airstairs weighed 500, so we were shipping 1,000 pounds back and forth with an empty container that weighed another 500 pounds.

We were needlessly carrying an empty container back and forth at great expense and I had an idea of how to rectify the problem but I couldn't get anyone to listen to me. Mr. Hall said, "I'm listening." My solution was to build six new aluminum containers and place them at all the major stations and leave the empty container there at that station. I pointed out; it would also be saving one half hour to have the inoperative stair already in the empty container ready to ship back to us.

He was flabbergasted to hear that we were shipping an empty container back and forth. He was so happy that I had brought this to his attention that he asked if there was anything else I could think of to help the airline. I gave him a total of eight items that needed to be looked into. When I left his office he shook my hand and said, "David, anytime you want to talk to me, you just call and tell them who you are and I'll make an appointment for you." My general foreman needed his shirt size increased by two sizes because his chest stuck out so far.

I was encouraged by that particular vice-president to come back and see him whenever I had an idea that could improve the company, which made me feel good. Two months later, six outside stations received brand-new, aluminum containers with instructions on the proper procedure for changing the stairs and leaving the empty boxes at the stations. This episode made my job easier and it also renewed my faith in the old saying: *It's the squeaky wheel that gets the oil.*

Winning A New Car

One distinct advantage of working for an airline was that I was able to fly home to see my mom, dad, sister and brothers several times a year. The only problem was not having access to a car at the other end, which meant renting or borrowing one. One time I was able to buy a 1960 Chevrolet and I made a deal with a very dear friend of mine's son, who had just turned sixteen and who jumped at the chance to take care of the car and drive it while I was not there. I have forgotten how long that lasted but it was fun and cheaper than renting a car.

When I was not able to rent one, my brother Doug would be kind enough to let me borrow one of his. Once, I remember, he told me to use one for as long I wanted. I asked him what was the occasion for his generosity and also what he planned to use. He told me he was going to the Packard factory to pick up a new car he had just won, and that he would be back in a couple of days and I could see it then.

While he was gone, I found out he had been telling the truth, and that out of 25,000 entries, he was one of the grand prize winners. The story appeared on the front page of the *Beverly Times*, as our local paper was called then. My brother had won by finishing the simple sentence: *I like the Packard automobile because…* in 25 words or less, but I never knew what his answer was and I wish I had kept the clipping to refer to. I was proud of him and I guess I have always styled my life after him. He was the one who turned Pa's store into a big supermarket and he was also the one there during its final days. I really don't know the reasons the store went out of business because I wasn't around.

Last Words

The last words in my first book, *Memoirs of a Little Italian Boy* were: "There is a Varga in my life, but that's another story...to be continued."

The Varga I write about is an airplane like none other. Les, a very close friend of mine, wanted us to become partners by buying a plane together. After selling both his Champ and mine we decided to follow up on an ad for a Varga in *Trade-a-Plane*, but it was all the way in Mississippi. I called the owner, who said that his Varga in mint condition, but both Les and I knew better than to expect that to be true.

We left early one morning and after nine hours of hard driving through Florida, I called ahead to the owner of the plane to be sure he knew we were coming and to arrange for him to meet us at the airport. He seemed happy we were nearly there, but had forgotten to mention one Airworthy Directive that had not been complied with on his plane. He said not to worry because he had ordered new parts for the engine and they would be there in the morning and then we could fly the plane home after it was fixed.

It seemed to me I'd heard that song before, which should automatically have thrown up a red flag for us. We looked at each other and decided to continue since we were only 30 minutes away and besides, the owner had my $1000 down payment.

We met him at the hanger and after introducing ourselves walked in to see the plane. Come to find out he was not the owner; he was the chief mechanic at the fix base operation and was speaking on behalf of the owner. To make matters worse, there on the floor lay the whole back of the engine in a puddle of dirty oil: gears nuts, bolts, accessory plates, the engine cowl—it was a mess.

We carefully looked over the rest of the plane, hoping to find something we could say made it worthwhile to have come so far, but could find nothing. I asked to borrow the logbooks to take back to the hotel room so that I could examine them, and then we left, tired and hungry. We had just about decided not to buy the plane but needed to sleep on it. I did look over the logs and was convinced it was not for us.

The next morning I returned his logbooks and he gave back my check. We were disappointed because we had come such a long way to find out that there were too many things wrong with the plane.

Back on the road in a blinding rainstorm at about 8:00 a.m. with wipers flapping, raindrops slapping, lightening flashing, and thunder clapping. About an hour went by before the sun shone through the clouds. During the drive, we spoke about another Varga that we had seen at Spruce Creek six months before. Its owner and I had played golf several times but he had never mentioned anything about selling his plane. It sounded very interesting, so I called him that night to find out more about the plane.

He said he was interested in selling it because he wanted something faster. I could tell by his appraisal of it that it was what we were looking to buy. He gave me a price that was firm and one we both agreed on and as far as I was concerned the plane was ours. The owner agreed to fly it to Daytona Beach in about three weeks.

On his flight to Florida he was forced to land in Savannah, because the plane had electrical problems. He left it with the Fix Base Operation to fix and he flew back to Daytona on a commercial flight. Two days later the FBO called and said his plane was ready. Now it was my chance to hitch a ride back with him, because a friend was going to fly him back to pick it up. We arrived in Savannah late the next morning and I couldn't wait to see this jewel. I always work myself up into a dither, anticipating the worst but still hoping for the best.

I practically ran through the office to get to the hangar door and fling it open , and there it was...like he said, the most beautiful Varga in the world. I wondered how we could be so lucky to find this one and it was in our own backyard all the time.

We test-ran the engine, the mechanics put the cowl on it and we were on our way. The ride back was delightful and I just sat in the back seat and enjoyed every minute of it. We did a few odd jobs that needed fixing and it was finally ours.

We formed a new company and licensed it under the name *Aircraft Positioning Systems, Inc.* Les was still working a regular job at the time and had only weekends off. When Saturdays came, I gave way to him because I could fly any day during the week. When Bruce, our third partner came into town, I would give way to him so that he could fly. In the meantime they both were building up a lot of time in formation flying and becoming very efficient. I tried flying formation for awhile and I enjoyed it, but it was not my idea of fun flying. I more enjoy going on Sunday excursions with Nancy to Titusville for breakfast, because the cook there makes good omelets.

SECTION TWO:
AROUND THE HOUSE

Twirling

When Nancy and I met, she lived in the Kendall Lakes Condo apartment complex, which consisted of side-by-side units, each with an up and a down stairs. We had no idea where any of the building plans were that would help us if we had trouble with electrical or plumbing problems, and of course you don't think about things like that when moving into a new place. Nancy had her unit fixed up quite nicely, with long mirrors on the narrow living room walls that made the room look much larger than it really was.

One of the many reasons I thought she was very interesting was that she had built a wooden step-up platform in the dining area. Hanging from the ceiling was a gray, seashell fabric that hung over the area like a tent with a light fixture hanging down in the middle. Here is the extraordinary touch. The base of the table was made from a huge tree stump that looked like it was growing out from the floor. On it was a large, round glass top.

The upstairs main bedroom was also unique and it had an eight-foot, round bed in the middle of it which I found very interesting. The large wall had a mural that was an autumn scene in New England. There was a second bedroom surrounded by closet space, and a second bath. Nancy had lived there for about five years before I came along and we married. We were far enough away from the main street that we were not able to hear traffic on Kendall Drive. Our backyard bordered on a canal and across from that was an open field, so we had no backyard neighbors.

One evening after dark we heard a commotion out back, and saw flashing lights, which is generally not a good sign. A lady had somehow driven right into the canal. When the police arrived on the scene, the officer dove into the water to get the driver out of the car. He kicked in the rear window and was able to save the lady from drowning. The ambulance took her away to the hospital; she was lucky to be alive. When the officer got back to his squad car where he had left his wallet and wristwatch on the front seat to keep them from getting wet, they were gone. There he stood in complete disbelief, soaking wet after saving the lady's life. That was only one of many exciting moments living there.

Occasionally, but not very often, we could hear our next-door neighbors through the walls. One day while we were away our neighbor's toilet became plugged up. He told me that he thumbed through the yellow pages and found the name of a plumbing company who had been in business for 20 years. Thinking that was a good recommendation for reliability, he called them for the job.

The plumbers arrived about 7:00 p.m. only to find that the owner did not have a schematic of the underground plumbing. They found what they thought was the correct plumbing access opening, but it was out in the middle of the street. The plumbers inserted an enormously long snake into the pipe as if they knew what they were doing. A plumbers' snake, for those who do not know it, is a long, round and flexible metal rod that is tightly wrapped on a reel and is strong enough and stiff enough to feed into a pipe and penetrate any obstruction that might be clogging the pipe.

The owner of the apartment, anxious to help, stationed himself upstairs and was prepared to yell out the window when the snake emerged from his toilet. He was ever so watchful, but after many minutes went by he became nervous. They had been pushing that great big long snake into the pipe for over ten minutes. He kept yelling from the bathroom window, "Nothing yet," to the workers below to let them know that the toilet was still plugged up. Suddenly they realized that they had pushed the gadget as far as it would go and they were getting nowhere, so they decided to pull it back out of the pipe and start all over again.

The harder they pulled on it, the harder it resisted and after 10 minutes of trying to pull it out, they decided to send one of the men up into the bathroom to see what was wrong. One man stayed on the ground and made the other go upstairs with the owner to watch for any indication of movement. When he got upstairs, he yelled through the window, "Try it again." He started the motor that turned the Roto-Rooter and suddenly the man upstairs yelled, "Stop!" He had heard something going on in the next apartment.

He came downstairs and went to the next apartment only to find the door locked and nobody home. As he started to leave the premises, the lady who owned the apartment came home and let him into her unit. As he started upstairs he noticed that water was running down the stairs and they both let out a scream.

The Roto-Rooter had come up into her bathroom because the two apartments were connected with a Y-fitting to save pipe material, and the snake came up into her side instead of his. Her toilet bowl was smashed. The snake had picked up the rug on the floor, smashed the sink, and was on its way through the shower doors and out the window to the roof.

I wonder if they would have stopped when the apartment started spinning off its foundation, or if they would have kept going until the roof fell on their heads.

The plumbers found later that all the apartments were connected by Y-joints but that practice was eventually discontinued. I shudder to think what might have happened if that lady next door had been home getting ready in the bathroom, doing whatever ladies do to get ready, and the snake had come through the toilet. There might have been a lot of screaming and yelling and it would not have been a pretty picture.

Author's note: I hope you are laughing as hard as I am while writing this. Not much of anything else happened while we lived there except that after one of the hurricanes blew down a large bougainvillea bush which blocked the front entrance to the front of the house, we were not able to get in the front door. There was no way through the sliding glass doors in the back so I spent about three hours removing thorny branches, piece by piece.

The Latest

When I wake up in the morning, I wonder: *What am I going to do today?* I might ask: *What is going to happen to me today?* if I were inclined to be a fatalist, but I'm not. My whole trick in life is to wake up feeling like I have everything under control and I am positive about my ability to handle anything that happens, good or bad. I just want to tell you, whatever you may think, that during moments of sheer delight and ecstasy, up jumps the devil and there isn't much you can do about it.

My story started about two months ago, maybe even three months. I'm really not sure. It is an insidious tale, one that I would have considered sending to Alfred Hitchcock if he were still alive.

For the life of me, I can't understand why our dog RB, which is short for Rhett Butler, would lie in certain places throughout our house. We think he's kind of kooky anyway, but being the alpha dog, he figures he has claim to certain spaces on the floor for his very own. Most dogs have a basket with a pillow in it for their very own. We have two dogs; we would have to have two baskets which would take up too much space, so we give them the whole house to choose from, except in our bed or on the furniture. They consider the whole floor as their domain, anyway.

RB has a favorite spot on the tile at the entrance to our kitchen. He is always in the way, lying there, and I have to step over him while hoping that I don't step on him. The same is true when I walk through the hall in the front of the house, which has nice cool tiles for him to lie on. The few times that I have walked through the house barefoot, I have noticed a warm spot where he has been.

The warm spots were the beginning of a strange happening I really didn't understand. I thought that I knew what was going on in every part of my house. You may think you know everything, but you don't. One day, when I happened to walk barefoot over that spot in the doorway of the kitchen, the spot seemed unusually warm. I figured RB had been there earlier and I just hadn't seen him. Then I noticed several more times that it was warm, and I knew he had not been there because he was outside most of the day.

I kept feeling a warm spot in that area, but dismissed it from my mind until one night. We went to bed about midnight, and it became extremely quiet in the house and I could hear a slight hissing sound like water was running somewhere. I got out of bed and walked into all the bathrooms. I heard the sound the loudest in ours. I couldn't find anything unusual there, so I went back to sleep.

Each day I looked for places where the sound might be coming from. I tried shutting off the main water supply in the garage which didn't make any difference: I could still hear the sound very faintly. Then I found that the main shut-off valve was not closing tightly, so that was a losing battle. I didn't have the proper tool to shut off the water at the meter, so I called Les for help as I usually do. He shut off the main valve near the street and we could still hear the sound. We were stymied.

I decided to call a leak detector company for advice. Two men came and looked over the situation and decided that either it was too much work or that they did not want the job. One said, "I wouldn't worry about it as long as your house doesn't float away." He charged me $125 for that brilliant statement and went on his way.

I was determined to do something, even if it was the wrong something. I called American Leak Detector Company and two men came with all kinds of instruments. It took them almost three hours to systematically trace where the water pipes were under the cement slab that this house was built on. He pointed to a spot in the middle of our living room, under the slab. He said, "It's right under the corner of the fireplace, it is right here," and he pointed to a spot. He gave me the names of four plumbing companies and I made an appointment with the first one on the list for the Tuesday after Christmas.

I've been a foreman over hundreds of men who knew their jobs and some who didn't, but even they had sense enough to ask how a job should be done. The plumber was careless when he was using the electric hammer, because when he was chopping the cement into small pieces, the hammer slipped and went right through the cold water line. This deluged him with cold water and luckily we had plastic covers over the rug behind him. He quickly stuck his finger over the hole while I ran out into the garage and shut off the water valve. It took him an hour to repair that mistake and another hour to fix the hot water line that had a pinhole in it.

In the process of cleaning up the area he overloaded the bucket with the broken pieces he had chipped out of the floor. When he lifted the heavy bucket, he hurt his back and was squirming on the floor in agony. I almost called 911 but he insisted he could manage the rest of the job. I helped him with the rest of the pieces of cement until he was able to mix new cement. He dumped that batch of new mix into the hole in the floor only to find out that it wasn't enough. He left, grumbling to himself, to get another bag of cement, more time wasted. On his return he was able to finish the job and to give me a bill.

We waited a couple of days, both for the cement to dry and for a rug man to secure the rug back onto the floor. When the job was finally finished, the rug put down and the furniture back in place, I was a complete wreck. The last time I had such a traumatic experience was when my cellar was flooded on a cold night in New England and it put out our furnace. We found out later that the cellar floor had been built a foot below the water table.

If you are still wondering why RB kept lying on that spot at the entrance to the kitchen, it was where the hot water line was always flowing under the slab on its way toward the leak.

Above Ground Level

It was the day after Christmas when Nancy and I took possession of our house at Spruce Creek Fly-in. I was still working at Eastern Airlines and Nancy had accepted a job at Deltona Middle School, which was to start the first of February. This was an exciting time in our life together, away from Miami and in our new house. We loved our new surroundings but didn't know much about them.

I asked the real-estate lady who had sold us the house if she knew anything about the sprinkler system. We wanted to water the grass because it had turned brown, which is normal in winter months. She didn't know anything about the house because it had only been on the market a couple of weeks. I finally found out that the water supply to the sprinklers was coming from city water. This seemed to me to be an expensive way to water grass.

Finally, the opportunity came for many homeowners who wanted to put in wells to do so at discount prices. When the well drillers came with their rig, they drove the main pipe down 125 feet and we had plenty of water. Then I found that the eight valves that control the sprinklers were deep in the ground and covered over with dirt. Whoever put them in buried them so deep it was almost impossible to work on them.

Whenever I manually turned the switch on for the front yard, the swimming pool began to fill with water. I couldn't imagine why my pool was always so full of water. It's funny but my dogs knew, because they barked anytime the pool started filling. The whole system seemed to be mixed up.

After going through every possible method of trouble shooting, I decided to take drastic steps to end this ridiculous dilemma. The main reason behind my decision was that it was difficult for me to lie on my belly and work on the valves deep in the ground. I was still mending from open heart surgery just five months earlier and this was not my favorite position. I thought back to when the doctor had told me to be careful and be sure to let my breast plate heal properly, because I wouldn't like the sound of it going *click, click* when I tried to sleep at night because the bones had not mended properly.

That's what made me decide to chop all the valves out of the ground and put in a whole new system, the way I wanted it to be. The hardest part was to dig up the dirt around each valve to have room enough to work around it. I cleared the dirt down to the top of each valve and then I dug big holes at each end of the excavation. I washed all the valves down with the garden hose until there was enough clearance all around them. After several washings they were all clear. Then I started to chop out each valve and I just did not believe how someone had put these pipes together to form this monstrosity.

Now I had the job of designing where and how the valves were going to be put aboveground. I finally put together eight valves in clusters of four, with pipes leading down into the ground like a small octopus, and I connected them to the water supply. After a few adjustments and with help from the barking dogs, the sprinkler system was finally in, aboveground and working the best it had ever worked.

As a professional touch, Nancy came up with the idea to have a decorative wishing well to cover the pipes, with access doors above the valves in case of emergency. We found a company out west that builds wishing wells out of redwood. We sent them the exact measurements that we needed to cover all the valves.

It took three weeks for them to build it and seven days over the road to deliver. It arrived in the back end of a semi in a blinding rainstorm, but was completely covered with plastic and braced on all four sides. The driver gently lowered it to the ground on his hydraulic tailgate and rolled it into the garage. It was a beautiful sight, far better than I had expected.

I came up with another bright idea and it was for a way for us to lift this 300-pound wishing well onto a pad that I had made for it to fit over the valves. Wednesday is my day to play golf with my friends, so after our group played the fourth hole, I talked them into driving their golf carts over to my house, which is just a stone's throw away from the fifth hole. The four of us, one on each corner, lifted the new wishing well up and on to the pad. There it now sits majestically, and we are so pleased. Mike was the first one to put a penny in the well and he made a wish. I hope your wish comes true, Mike.

It Happens Every Time

Whenever we're getting ready to go on vacation, I usually wait until the last minute before I cut the grass just so that it won't be knee-high when we get back. Rain was predicted during the time we were to be away in South Florida. So I grabbed my gas can and headed for the back yard, where my super lawnmower resides under a shelter that I made to keep the rain off it. After filling the two front tires with air, and the gas tank with gas, it was ready to go.

I jumped on the seat just like a cowboy jumps on his horse, slammed in the brake and clutch, turned the key to start—and the *tur-r-r-r* sound did not happen. The sound was more like *we-e-e-e* and again *we-e-e-e*. I said, "Oh, Oh," and a few chosen words and jumped off the mower. I proceeded to lift up the cover to investigate what the hell had happened and decided to tear into it and find out.

I was standing under the roof of the shelter, bent over because of the height of the roof and getting cramps in my back. I decided to push the mower backwards out from under the shelter so that I didn't have to bend.

I finally got all the parts off and out of the way and I could see the problem. The starter Bendix was broken. This is a part of the starter that helps it to engage the engine and then release when the engine starts. So I put all the parts into a container, spread a piece of plastic over the open engine and closed the hood down and left it right there.

One week later, after arriving back from vacation, I called an 800-number and I ordered a new part for the starter. The salesman promised that it would be delivered to our house in three days. It was going to be rainy for the next two days so I wouldn't be able to work on it anyway. After all the bad weather passed the new parts arrived on time and I went to work on the starter. Getting the starter off was kind of tricky but I've had harder jobs.

I've stopped for a moment to make a title change. I'm renaming the end of this story right here and it's going to be called: *The World Has Come to an End because of a C-Clip.*

A C-clip is shaped just like the letter C and is generally made of wire spring steel. The steel shaft has a groove at the top for the clip to snap into which holds all the parts together. The steel shaft is about the diameter of a pencil and is only three inches long. Without this clip to lock all the parts in place, the mechanism is useless.

The parts that I ordered were in the box and nothing was missing except the tool to take the C-clip off and another tool to put it back on. I had neither tool at my disposal but because of my years as a mechanic I would find a way to get this C-clip on. I had no trouble getting the old clip off but putting the new clip on was another story. I tried every method I knew to get that dumb clip on and decided they were right: I had to have the tool.

I called the 800-number again and got a nice lady who looked up the part number and said she would have to order the tool from the manufacturer. In the meantime, during the conversation with her, I could hear my grass growing even faster. She said that the tool would take at least ten days and cost $19.00 and another seven bucks to ship it. By this time my grass was screaming. I told her to hold off on the order until I gave it some thought. I called Les Lowman, who was my partner in a Varga airplane and who had saved me many times over. I told him the situation and he came to see what was needed. I had the picture of the tool on the parts list and explained to him how it worked, and he said, "I'll look for some material to make it out of and I'll see you later."

I figured tomorrow would be the earliest I would see him. Fifteen minutes later he knocked on my kitchen door and handed me a plastic tube with a brand new stainless steel tool in it, and we tried it and it fit right over the shaft. We carefully placed the C-clip on the motor shaft and give it a whack and on it went and the world started turning again.

I can't praise Les enough for all the things he has done for me and for many others in our community. That is why our community is so unique: Here people help people.

I Feel A "Coal" Coming On

When summer is over and leaves start to fall, there is much to be done to clean up the mess. The only way to pick up all the leaves is to use a lawn mower that acts as a vacuum cleaner. Also the pool deck is usually covered with mildew and has to be bleached and that's a big job. I can only do some of these things when the spirit moves me and when the weather is good.

It took me two hours of hard work to clean the pool furniture. It was in bad shape with mildew, sand and dirt, and the cleaning was long overdue. When the job was finished all the rags and bucket had to be stored back in the garage. I went back through the gate to the rear of the house and pulled the 50-foot hose to the front of the house where it is stored and I remembered to shut off the water. The mailman had just stopped and dropped off a package with the rest of the mail. Soaking wet with sweat, and anxious to get my clothes off and into the washer, I didn't waste any time going to the rear of the garage. The first things I took off were my wet shoes, socks and black pants, which were stinky from the bleach I had been using on the furniture.

All of the black stuff went into the washer along with socks and pants from my closet and another pair of black pants that needed washing. Loaded with soap, the old machine started chugging as if to say: *That's enough for one load.* With that all in progress, I went into the kitchen to cool down a bit before taking a shower. With a very thirsty mouth, I got a glass out of the cabinet, put a piece of ice in it, filled it with root beer, took a sip and then decided to have a cookie. I do have a bad habit when I am hungry; I have a tendency to cram things into my mouth. The cleaning lady had been at our house the day before, so

I crammed the whole cookie in my mouth so that no crumbs would fall on the floor. As I was standing there in my undershorts and shirt, I heard a knock at the door.

As the door opened from the garage, I peeked around the corner and saw Eleanor, a very close friend, herding our dogs back into the house. I was unable to speak because I had the cookie in my mouth, petrified because I couldn't step out and greet her because I didn't have enough clothes on and mad at the dogs but couldn't scold them. As I stood there, still hiding behind the wall, she went on to explain that she was driving by our house when she saw one dog in the middle of the street and the other in the driveway. She stopped and brought them in because she knew they weren't supposed to be out there. I mumbled, "Thanks," to her the best I could with my mouth full, and after she left, I decided to retrace my steps to find out how they got out.

I thought back to pulling the long hose up to the front of the house, and remembered that when I had shut off the water, I had not gone back to close the gate. Many times before, as long as I was around to watch the dogs, they had never dared to come out. When I went in the house, they saw their chance to go on a wild adventure. All they needed were long sticks with bags hung on the end of them, full of sandwiches, slung over their shoulders. They could have gone on a hiking trip down by the creek or to the runway, to watch airplanes take off and land, having a merry old time. Isn't it strange that this should happen so close to Christmas when those who have been bad get a stocking full of coal? Now I ask you, whom do you think should get the coal stocking this year: the dogs, or me?

Out Of Sync

It was a bright and sunny day and I was driving to the grocery store. As always, I had a mental inventory of what I needed at the store and was happy in the thought that I remembered to take my grocery list and money. Suddenly, I realized that I had forgotten to grab extra money on the way out of my house. I certainly did not have enough in my pocket to buy groceries, so I needed to go back home.

I slammed on the brakes to turn the car around. I felt like an idiot, but luckily there was a driveway just ahead and no other cars in sight. The way was clear for me to make a turn into that driveway. As I approached it, I noticed that it was wider than most driveways. It was also comforting to know that it would save me time, not have to go all the way around the block. Slowly I turned my car into the driveway and stopped. I looked around a little before putting my car in reverse. Then, when I was ready to back up, I looked in the rearview mirror and with great surprise; there right behind me, waiting to turn into his driveway, was the owner of the house. I couldn't believe it, where in hell had he come from? Hurriedly I backed out of his way and in the wrong direction. He didn't leave me enough room to turn in the right direction, which was the reason I was turning around in the first place.

In my haste to get out of his way, I almost knocked down his mailbox. I just nodded to him as if to say, *I'm sorry that I got in your way*, and drove farther down the street and found a safe place to make a U-turn. Driving as far to the right as possible, I accidentally ran off the road onto someone's lawn. When I did, I heard a thud. I looked back in the mirror, and saw the remains of what used to be a toy. Some kid must have left his little scooter too close to the road and I had mangled it.

Just then, the man whose kid owned the toy heard the noise and came running out of his house. He had a pen in one hand and was writing my license number on the palm of his other hand. Of course, I couldn't get away then so I had to go back and pay for the damage. I met the man in the middle of the street and, with a sheepish smile on my face I pulled out the last check from my checkbook.

I certainly didn't think it would cost any more than $25 to replace the toy. But he smiled and said, "I just paid $99 dollars for that hunk of junk, which used to be my son's scooter." I had no choice but to pay what he asked. At this point, I had completely forgotten why I was going back to my house and I continued on my way to the store.

I was about halfway there when my car started to shake like it was on a washboard road. I pulled over to see what was wrong and, sure enough, the noise was coming from the right front tire: It was flat. I wondered where I could have punctured it and realized that the scooter must have had something sharp sticking up. I did not get upset because I knew that getting the tire fixed would not be a problem. I had just renewed our AAA membership, so I called them directly from my cell phone. It was then that I found out that my wife was the only one who could use the card because we did not have a family membership.

I was still not discouraged because I knew that I could change the darn thing myself. After all, I had managed a gas station for five years and had owned cars for more than 60! I wasn't going to let a little thing like a flat tire stop me. After 20 minutes of rummaging around in the trunk of my car, I finally found the jack and read the directions on how to use it. I felt I was being really smart because I jacked the car up just high enough so that the flat tire was barely touching the ground, in case the wheel nuts were hard to loosen. After more searching, I found the wrench to loosen the nuts but it was so small that it would have worked better on a bicycle. I tried it anyway, but couldn't turn the nuts loose. Just about that time, along came a friend who stopped to help. He too, tried my wrench to no avail, and then he went to his car and got his own. That one didn't work either, but he also located a piece of pipe about three feet long in the back of his car and we made an extension for more leverage and that did it.

Between the two of us, we got the wheel off. I dragged the spare out of the compartment only to find that it was flat. I was still not too upset because my friend drove me and the spare to a gas station to put air in it.

He dropped me off at the station and I talked the station manager into driving me back to my car to put the tire on. The station manager finished the job and I continued to the store.

After an hour of shopping and gossiping with friendly neighbors, I was relaxed because I had found everything on my list and I had a full cart of groceries. I was also pleased because there was no one ahead of me in the checkout line. Just as I reached the cashier, my memory snapped into gear; I never had gone back for my wallet. I was now faced with another dilemma: Should I call my wife at work to bring some money, or just put everything on hold and drive back to get my wallet? I decided it would be best just to drive back, but first I had to put the ice cream and other frozen foods back into the freezer.

As I trudged empty-handed through the parking lot, I muttered about things happening for the best. I should have known better. I located my car and headed for home. As I was leaving the parking lot, I could see cars coming in the far distance. The roadway near me was clear, so I stomped hard on the accelerator and neglected to come to a full stop at the stop sign. I shouldn't have done that, because waiting for me just down the way was a very nice-looking policeman on a motorcycle. I knew I couldn't outrun him, so I had to stop. Then, like a sledge hammer, the thought hit me. My license, along with all my money, was in the wallet at home.

Excuses were running rampant in my head. Should I tell the policeman all the things that had happened to me, in hopes of changing his mind about writing a citation? In my heart I knew he wouldn't really want to hear them, so I resigned myself to accept my fate quietly. Just as he walked up to my car with his book in hand to write a ticket, two kids went speeding by in another car. Without hesitating, he turned and got on his motorcycle and went racing after them. I reasoned that since he no longer cared whether I stayed, I had no reason to wait. I took advantage of this wonderful opportunity and continued on my way home to get my wallet. Only this time, I knew how lucky I was.

As I approached my house, I noticed that I had company. There, parked in front of my driveway, was the car that had been speeding and the same police motorcycle. The policeman was writing a speeding ticket for the kids who must live nearby. I figured that there was no sense in stopping at my house this time around, so I just drove on by and counted my blessings. It had been one of those days when I was out of sync with the world. I decided right then, that I'd better get back in sync immediately.

I drove slowly around the block and by the time I arrived back at my house, the police officer and the kids were gone. I drove into my driveway and put the car away in the garage. Then I felt safe. I did not go back to the store until the next day.

It Won't Fall Very Far

When the world seems to fall down around you, it won't fall very far. The early morning sun is just peeking through the trees and somehow you know it's going to be a great day. Breakfast time is usually pretty thrilling for me, because I have a chance to show Nancy how wonderfully I can cook eggs any way that she likes them. There's nothing I like better than to have her sit down and eat my special eggs on a pre-sliced-in-half, gluppy-mayonnaise covered slice of honey wheat, 40 calories, with a square piece of fat-free American cheese, sliced down the middle, each half on top of the hot steaming scrambled eggs. Then the call goes out: "It's ready, honey." Then I eat breakfast with my beautiful wife: Who could ask for anything more? She then goes happily off to work while I finish washing the dishes.

One particular day I noticed that the water was slowing down coming out of the faucet. All the faucets in the house were plugged up with a white chalky substance that comes from calcium in the hot water tank. I took them all apart and cleared them so that I could shave and shower to continue my morning routine.

A storm was brewing, but I had to make a hurried trip to the clubhouse to pay a bill. On my way back I was caught in a cloudburst, with lightening and thunder, and it was really scary. It was almost impossible to see ahead but I kept driving carefully so as not to run off the road. I hurried as fast as I could because I know that my dogs go crazy barking during a thunder storm. When I drove into the garage, the power in my house suddenly went off. When this happens, the electric garage door will not operate, so I had to leave it open. The storm intensified and the wind was swirling leaves and rain into the garage. I decided to manually close the door, and so I pulled the emergency chain to unlock it and the door came crashing down and hit the floor with a loud bang. I had no idea why it did that, but I found out later that one of the overhead springs that helps ease the door down had broken.

Ruth's caregiver, Jutta, called me in the middle of all this confusion to tell me that the roof was leaking at Mom's house from all the rain. I told her I would be right there to see what I could do to solve the problem. I put two flashlights and some towels into my car and then tried to manually open the garage door but couldn't lift it.

I immediately called overhead doors for help and told them of my dilemma, because I couldn't get out of my garage. I told the man that I had to get to my mother-in-law's house because her roof was leaking. I was talking to him on the house phone about the garage door when Nancy called on my cell phone and was telling me to go right away to mother's house because the roof was leaking. I had a phone stuck in each ear, trying to direct the conversation into the right one.

The man interrupted several times to tell me that there was a lot of static on the line, which I already knew. He kept saying that he couldn't hear a word I was saying and it was because I wasn't talking to him on his phone at the time. I tried to explain to Nancy and said, "Honey, I can't leave because the garage door won't open to get my car out," and the man must have thought I was calling him honey. Finally, I heard him say, "Are you also talking on a cell phone? Because it's causing too much interference and I can't hear you." So I told Nancy the man couldn't hear me so I had to hang up. While I was getting ready to hang up the phone, I heard Nancy tell me to ask Lisa, who lives across the street, if she would drive me up to Mother's. I felt that it wouldn't help if she took me to Mother's because there had to be someone here when the garage door man came. He heard some of the conversation on the other phone and said, "What?"

I hung up the cell phone and immediately called John across the street to take me to Mom's house. We went to Mom's and saw that the situation was under control because she had pans to catch the water coming through the ceiling.

We left there almost immediately and arrived back home in time to see Nancy pull into the driveway. She unloaded Mom's flowers from her car, loaded towels back into her car to help dry up water on her floor, and off she went. She called ten minutes later to say that we were not going out to dinner after all and to just relax.

I'm sure that my blood pressure went sky high because I was huffing and puffing, when she said, "Relax." You just never know when "the fit is going to hit the shan" and come tumbling down around you.

Sub note: During all the confusion, I did have time to shower, shave, and shampoo and get all dressed and ready to go out to Woody's. At that moment, I wondered if George, Nancy's dad, was looking down at us, laughing his ass off.

The story goes on from there because after sopping up most of the dripping water, they discovered why the roof was leaking. The next day the roofing man found that one of the workers had forgotten to install about a 10-foot-long weather strip that should have been put down when they put on the new roof after the hurricane. So all is well and things are almost back to normal, but I think George is still laughing. Isn't it funny: It was kind of hard to make him laugh while he was here, but not anymore--because I can hear him clearly now.

Work That's Never Done

It never rains but it pours. When I think of May 18, 2009, I will always remember how, in the previous five days, it had rained a total of 22 inches, which is far more than it typically does during a hurricane. Normally, we don't have to worry about flooding because we are 25 feet above sea level. Drainage has not been my primary thought for the past 23 years because I make sure our roof gutters and downspouts are all clear. I know that they are connected to flex pipes under the ground which are designed to carry all the rain water from the roof to the property line and down over the embankment to the creek.

I have not been in close contact with work around the house for the past several months because you might say my age is slowing me down. So as a result, I have not kept my eye on things like I used to.

On one of my walks around the yard checking on things, I noticed an unusual dip in the ground near the fence, where the water from the roof empties and trickles down to the creek. After a closer inspection, I could see undercutting outside the fence, like an animal had been digging.

So I climbed around the fence, stepped on what looked like solid ground and stopped short of falling into a big hole. Unknown to me for all of the years we had been living in this house, the rain water coming off the roof had been dribbling down in the same spot, gradually washing away the dirt from ground level until the top soil finally gave way. This exposed a trench five feet wide; with only the tree roots I was standing on holding the sides together. The bottom of the washout was about ten feet below where I was standing. Needless to say, I cautiously stepped back onto solid ground.

Obviously, immediate action was necessary before any more damage was done. I was losing part of my property into a *sinkhole*. After several sleepless nights, I decided to seek help. It came in the form of a worker with muscle to spare. We hooked 40 feet of additional flexible, plastic pipe to the two shorter pipes that were already installed. Before we could fill in the hole, it started raining again. However, at least the water was being directed down over the hill and closer to the creek. About a week later, when the weather cleared, I ordered two truck loads of fill dirt to replace the damaged ground.

I'm just thankful that it was caught in time because it could have been much worse. I might have had to write a whole SECTION about how my house was swallowed up by a sinkhole. Now I can breathe a whole lot easier, but I will still keep one eye in that direction.

SECTION THREE:
ANIMAL ANTICS

What's That Noise?

You know that things must be getting bad, when it rains every day and the grass is growing so fast that it makes funny sounds and it keeps me awake at night. That's the way it has been for the past few weeks. I'm not the type to complain about having to cut the grass, because I do have a rider lawn mower, which makes it very easy for me to zip around the yard in an hour. But when it rains every day it makes it impossible to mow because the grass is so wet. I strategically plan to do it, when it becomes dry enough.

I waited seven or eight days before I decided to make a run at it. A lot has to happen before I can even think about starting the mower, because most times the tires are flat and sometimes the battery is dead and I have to recharge it overnight, which postpones the mowing for one more day. I came in the house and changed into my work clothes and shoes because mowing is a very dusty and dirty job. Then I moved the portable air tank nearer the compressor and filled it with 100 pounds of air. That does not make the portable tank weigh 100 pounds; it just means that the air is compressed to 100 pounds. Then I brought the portable air tank to the mower and filled the tires to their proper pressure which only took a few minutes, but it meant bending down and getting into an awkward position. It wasn't so bad, but there are times when I battle spiders hanging from my nose and down in my shirt which causes some excitement.

I took the three grass-catching containers off the back end of the mower in preparation to pump up the tires and it was a good thing that I did because when I stooped down to put air in the tires I saw the long tail end of a snake slither up over the tire and disappear. I stopped in my tracks because I didn't want an encounter with a snake while I was mowing the grass. I couldn't tell what kind it was because it happened so fast.

I went back into the house and got a flashlight and shined it all over the mower but to no avail. Since I could not see the snake, I figured that he was scared off or just hiding, so I pumped up the flat tires. I went around to the front end and got on the mower, started the engine and backed out as fast as I could and jumped off and left it running. I looked it all over again, thinking that if he was still hiding in or around the mechanism I was going to give him the ride of his life.

I pushed full throttle, let out the clutch and screamed around the lawn, and completed cutting grass in record time, and he still didn't show himself. I don't know what snakes do in situations like that but if he survived the ride that I gave him, he's probably back in his nest telling his buddies what a wild ride he just took with a Little Italian Boy.

When I think back to all the times I have jumped on that mower without even looking it over for snakes, I shudder to think what might have happen if one popped out in front of my nose while I mowed around the pool. We might both have gone swimming. So from now on, I must make a snake check before entering into the wild kingdom of my backyard.

Not To Be

This is a story about a dog. I can't tell you in plain terms what a dog means to a family like ours, but it takes precedence over us humans. Our family includes two of the most delightful Shelties, who are brother and sister from the same litter. This is the second set of Shelties we have had, and they have completely different personalities than the others.

There is something special about these dogs, and not just because they are ours. Shelties are herders. Their devotion to us as owners is uncompromised, because they not only take care of each other but of us, too. I would not care to have any other breed. This is our kind of dog. They have a lot of fur that requires constant grooming, hearty personalities, beautiful colors and they are what we love.

This is a lead-in for a story about another dog we had occasion to deal with. After the death of their beloved Bichon Frise, Mom and Dad hungered to find another dog as lively, loving and devoted. As fate would have it, Nancy's sister found a Bichon Frise puppy that needed a home and she walked into the house and surprised them with it one day.

It landed in Nancy's dad's lap with all the frivolity, fuzziness and love that a puppy can muster and George's first words were, "Oh my God." The dog went from lap to lap and was licking each of us as she went as if she couldn't get enough attention. It became evident that this dog was going to be a handful to train because it was a very energetic puppy with teeth and claws as sharp as razors. It wasn't long before we realized that it needed continual attention and discipline. She had several play toys to chew on, which weren't enough, because the table and chair legs seemed more inviting, though not as tasty as an old, ratty, squeaky, green cloth doll she always went back to. As if that were not enough, the many green plants that were close to the floor made tasty morsels to chew on, but in this house they were forbidden fruit.

By the end of the first day many questions had to be answered. We put our heads together to find a solution for training this "stick of dynamite". Her sleeping cage turned out to be her home away from home. The food seemed to agree with her but gave her too much energy, we could tell by the way she ran around biting everything that moved and everything that was only thinking of moving.

Each day was more of a challenge than the day before until it was finally decided that the dog was too much for Mom and Dad to manage. The dog needed a new home where it could be cared for and properly trained.

Nancy took the dog to our home and advertised for a new owner in *The News-Journal*. As luck would have it, the first party who called seemed desperate for that kind of a dog and begged us to hold it until they could get there to see it. That night the lady and a friend came to our house. They seemed to fall in love with the puppy. After reassuring us that it was a dog they would love, they bought it with the dog cage and all the food and drove off happy.

Forty-five minutes later the phone rang. It was the lady begging us to take the dog back because her husband wouldn't let her in the house. She was on the verge of tears. I'm not sure whether she was more worried about getting her money back, or about whether her husband would ever let her back into the house again.

She brought it back that same night and very unceremoniously I carried the heavy cage into the house, along with all the food and toys that went with the dog. I kept my teeth tightly clenched together so as not to say what was on my mind.

The dog was once again back in our care, barking louder than ever because she was so happy to be back in our half-friendly home. Somehow we managed to get through the night without too many interruptions. The next day, after much thought and discussion we called Nancy's sister, Alma. She called the previous owner, who was willing to take the dog back because the older dog she owned was pining away for the puppy.

Our house is quiet again, our dogs have stopped barking and raising hell and things seem to be back to normal. Thank heaven for our little Shelties who have each other to play with and us to love.

No More, Please

You would think that because of all that has happened to us, before, during and after my operation, that life would become a little easier and not one catastrophe after another. It's a good thing we cannot see into the future because there could be more in store for us that we don't know about. I'm not complaining, but it does seem as though our plates are full all the time, so things should be slowing down.

It was one of the days during my recuperation, three weeks after surgery. I was slowly getting my strength back but was still a little wobbly. It seemed that I was making fairly good progress. Nancy stayed strong during all this time, taking good care of me and she didn't need any added responsibilities. She had been fulfilling my every need and doing housework, cooking, washing, bringing work home and making sure I took all of my pills on time.

Getting to bed seemed the hardest thing for us to do, because my sleeping habits had changed since the operation. I had to continue to sleep on my back to make sure my breast bone healed together. My doctor had convinced me that I would not want to hear click, click from a not-healed-together breast bone. I had tried to start the night in bed but after about an hour I gave up. I then tried to sleep sitting up on the couch, where I could get occasional naps and that seemed to hold me together.

One night I went through my regular routine and was up again in an hour. I went to the couch but I don't remember how much time had passed before Nancy came into the room. She woke me and said, "There is a mouse in the wall again." We did have two mice in the wall several years back. The worst of that episode was that they died in there and the smell was intolerable. We tore down the part of the wall where we thought they were, and sure enough they were in there. After getting them removed the smell went away in a few days.

Well, here we were in the same situation, a mouse in the wall and me hopelessly incapable of doing anything about it in my condition. Only this time Nancy wanted to get the mouse out of there, not only to save its life and but to avoid the smell that might occur afterwards.

She couldn't sleep in the bedroom with the mouse scratching in the wall just behind her head, so she moved into the middle bedroom to go to sleep. She didn't get enough sleep to sustain her through the next day and it was starting to take its toll.

The next morning I called the POA office to find someone who could help as a handyman and do some of the things I would ordinarily be able to do. Luckily, a man whose name is Todd said he would help in any way we needed him. I made arrangements for him to come that afternoon when Nancy got home so that she could supervise the operation. After two, hard hours of cutting four holes in the wall down near the floor; he went into the attic through a trapdoor in the ceiling. After looking for a place the mouse might have fallen into, he came down and tried one more thing. He removed the light lens on the bathroom side of the wall and still found nothing. He finally, reluctantly, gave up and said there was nothing more he could do and left. At that point, Nancy did not want to give up and tried to come up with a solution to get the mouse out of the wall.

You must understand that Nancy loves animals. She always had pets of all kinds in her Media Center during her teaching years, for the kids to see and learn about—even some mice, so she knows a lot about them.

All during this time she kept hearing scratching coming from the wall but up a little higher than where Todd had been cutting. She wasn't going to let this mouse get the best of her, so she picked up a keyhole saw and started in an entirely new place, much higher up on the wall. She had carefully thought out how to cut into the wall without hitting anything. After about half an hour she had a small opening, about four inches square, between a vent pipe and the partition. Still no sign of the mouse.

She decided to take a chance that the mouse would climb a ladder made out of a cloth belt which she knotted in the part she put inside the wall. She left about two feet hanging out of the hole and into a plastic bucket. She said that if he fell into it he wouldn't be able get out. That all sounded well and good, since I don't know mice like she does. We walked back to the den to sit down because I was unable to stand any longer.

About ten minutes went by. Nancy heard scratching coming from the bedroom and went to investigate. She came back in the den with a smile on her face and said, "Come look" and there she had the mouse in the bucket. She was laughing and crying at the same time, saying, "We got him!" It was as if this were breathing new life and energy into her. She happily took the bucket out of doors and turned the mouse loose into the woods. She was still laughing and hugging me at the same time and when she went to bed that night she slept like a log. I never doubt anything she says that she can do. I never did before and I certainly won't start now.

Thinking Fast

There may come a time when you will have to think and act fast or be left way behind. Such a situation happened to me at the beginning of our trip to Boston. My wife and I were at the Daytona Beach International Airport. We had been through security, and were already on board the flight that was to take us to Cincinnati, where we were to change planes for Boston. We were going there to celebrate my brother, Joe's 95th birthday party the next day. Our luggage was on board and the carryon bags were in an overhead compartment when word came from the cockpit that our flight was canceled because of a mechanical problem.

This meant we would miss our connecting flight in Cincinnati and would not get in to Boston that day. That really is no way to start a vacation, even though, having been an airline mechanic for Eastern Airlines for 32 years, I know such problems happen. Nancy and I have had all kinds of things occur on flights, which makes us wonder what to do next: Roll with the punches, sit in the terminal and wait for something to happen, or do something about it, even if it's wrong. When something like this happens all you can do is try not to panic.

One lady did that, when it was announced that the flight was canceled: She let out a bloodcurdling scream and wanted off that plane and as far as I know, she was not going to get on another flight. Nancy, being the fast-thinking person that she is, took off through the terminal in search of a phone to call the airlines, to get us on another flight.

On her way to the phone she passed a gate that had a flight leaving for Atlanta in 15 minutes. She asked the agent if they had room for us on that flight. After explaining to the agent that our flight had been cancelled, they put us on board this one, with all our baggage, and we were on our way. We have no idea what happened to the other 40 passengers or even whether they got out that day. We made our connection in Atlanta and arrived in Boston, 30 minutes earlier than we would have on the other flight. This just adds to the many reasons I married Nancy 24 years ago, not only is she beautiful, but she is smart and fast thinking. I am pretty lucky, wouldn't you say?

For our rental car, we were fortunate to get a Ford van, which was fine for carrying our luggage. We headed toward Peabody, where my brother Joe lives in a new, assisted-living facility. I will not discuss here, for terror of retribution, the drivers in Massachusetts, because I have stated in previous writings that they are the world's *most unusual* drivers. Since I am originally from Beverly, MA I have an automatic driving mode: No matter where I am, all I have to do is push the button marked Boston. I just blend right in: It's scary but it works.

Joe's celebration was a tearjerker for him because all of his childhood girl and boy friends were there, along with 20 family members. Everybody had a good time. On Sunday we went on a whale-watching boat ride out of Gloucester. We tried to get Joe to go with us but it's not his thing. When we got back, we had lobster rolls for lunch. Later, Joe showed us around Brooksby Village, where he lives, and I must say there is every convenience available to all the people. I met two of my classmates who live there, and we had a nice reunion.

After spending three days at Joe's, we headed for western Massachusetts and on to Vermont to see Laura Govoni and Janice Hayes. They were the two ladies who came to my first book signing at Books-a-Million. They both are doctors of pharmacology and have written many books on the subject, the first of which is about three inches thick and is still used today by pharmacists everywhere.

The ladies explained to us that Laura wrote everything longhand and Janice typed it into manuscript form, and then it was submitted to the board for approval. I value their knowledge and their ability to write about such a difficult subject and put it into the annals of medicine.

Laura and Janice took us to a delightful dinner and a sightseeing tour of the town of Bennington, of which they are very proud. We spent the evening talking about the possibility of being related, had a restful night's sleep, and were on our way the next morning after a breakfast made in heaven by Janice.

We spent two days exploring Vermont. During one of those days we were screaming down one hill and up another when out popped a moose in front of our van. We were going about 50 mph and I had all I could do to stop from hitting it. I pulled to the side of the road and Nancy jumped out and tried to get a picture of it. The last I saw of her was with her arms flailing, and she was yelling, "Come back here, you moose."

While she was gone, I was looking in the car mirror to make sure that no one hit us in the rear end, when I saw another moose crossing the road behind us. I yelled to Nancy, who was coming out of the woods, but she couldn't hear me because all the windows in the van were closed. It, too, ran into the woods, but Nancy decided not to chase that one so we didn't get any pictures.

We drove off down the road with Nancy chuckling for about 30 minutes. She had seen her animals, which made the whole trip worthwhile.

SECTION FOUR:
ENCOUNTERS WITH PEOPLE

Fighter Pilot On Reconnaissance

He spoke with a low and quiet voice, and I could not have known he had been to hell and back. This was the first time we were paired up to play golf. I was interested to see how he hit the ball because I knew he was a few years older than I. He stood relaxed over the ball and with very little effort got tremendous distance out of it. You might say, *Hell, he hardly hit it.* The last I saw of the ball was when it blended into the white clouds above.

I got up in the same casual manner and took a bead on that white pro staff with a black dot and hauled off on it with a good smack. Funny when we both arrived at our respective hits, his was five yards further than mine. *How could this be?* I asked myself. As we walked from hole to hole I could tell he tired very easily and walked slower as time passed. We finished nine holes and were both happy in the thought that we were able to play golf at all.

I was able to ask about his background, like where he was from and what we did in life. We started talking about the war and some of the things that were funny and the things that were not so funny. He was five years older than I, which accounts for all his experience in flying.

He had been in the big war, WWII, and when I mentioned that I had been in the Navy, we both had things to talk about. He was small in stature and moved smoothly with each step, like someone who knew where he was going. When we started playing golf, his swing seemed smoother than mine but the ball went further and it's probably because I'm always trying to kill the ball.

The following week I found out that he had a story to tell and I'll convey it to you. He was a reconnaissance pilot in the Navy and flew in an F4F, which was a completely reconstructed fighter plane but had no armament and no guns. The company that manufactured it as a special project for the Navy installed larger fuel tanks so that it could stay aloft for seven hours.

On one particular recon mission he took off from his carrier and was gone for about five hours. When he returned to land on his carrier it was on fire because the Japanese had attacked it and it was severely damaged and he could not land. It was the Hornet at the battle of Midway.

He got permission to land on another carrier and they were going to push his plane overboard after he landed, because they said that they did not have enough room to keep it on board. He pleaded with them to refuel it so he could take off again, which they did. He headed northeast and was able to land at another naval air station on a string of islands in the Pacific and refuel again. He finally made it back to Pearl Harbor with nearly empty tanks.

As history has it, the Hornet was finally sunk off the coast of Santa Cruz Island on October 27, 1942, after taking severe punishment from Japanese dive bombers.

I finally convinced him to let me write his story for him after the Christmas holidays. I'm sorry to say that his story will never again be told by him because he passed away just months later.

Give Me Liberty

I think back to the very beginning, during my childhood, when I got my first plane ride in an open-cockpit, side-by-side, stick-controlled Spartan and just yesterday, 72 years later, I flew the latest developed aircraft, called the Liberty. They are so new that orders are being taken to buy them because they are so easy to fly. It certainly was a wakeup call to hear from a friend, who is the Southeast representative for the company, asking me if I wanted to fly. I had come back from a week's vacation on the west coast of Florida with my beautiful wife Nancy, and was resting my half-asleep body which came to life in an instant.

"You mean right now," I shouted.

"I mean right now," he said.

"I'll be there in five minutes," I shouted with glee and hung up the phone.

The hangar is six minutes away but I made it in five. It is the most beautiful plane in the world, the Liberty. I stood in awe, looking over this fine machine and it took my breath away. Everything about it seemed streamlined and slick with no rough edges to catch my shirt on or stub my toe. The owner took my picture standing posed looking at the rudder and the tail of the plane. He told me to get in the left seat if I was going to fly this airplane. This was the first airplane I had to be told how to get into. I clambered up onto the front of the leading edge of the wing in a sitting position and slid back about one foot where I was able to swing my feet into the cockpit and slide into the seat. It was new and different but easy and I am sure I will be more graceful the next time. I sat facing the latest technology on the instrument panel.

I was in a trancelike state, familiarizing myself with the instrument panel, more beautiful than any I had seen. I know it sounds like love at first sight, but that's the way it is about us pilots when we talk about airplanes.

I snapped out of the trance when my friend casually started the checklist of things to do to get that beauty started. It was as if I were in command of a magic carpet, as I told my thumb to push lightly on the throttle and adjust the right and left brake with the next two fingers, which I do not know the names of because I was still slightly mesmerized by the quick response my two fingers had on the controlled direction steering.

Before I knew it, we were on the runway centerline, lifting off in such a graceful motion that it seemed silly for me to sit there and say that I was flying this plane. It was flying itself and I just had my hands on the controls. All I had to do is think about where I wanted it to go and it went. We landed at three different airports and took off again, then came back home to Spruce Creek. This Liberty airplane is indeed a finely- tuned instrument of flight and will be in the air a long lifetime.

When The Chips Are Down

I really never know what's going to happen on any given day and this day started out to be pretty nice, so I just decided to go and hope for the best. I picked up George, Nancy's dad, and headed downtown. Our usual trek is to Dunkin Donuts. After critiquing all the bad drivers and why they don't use turn signals, we stop and settle down at our favorite coffee shop. There are some days that I think we might be in the middle of a demolition derby when we enter the parking lot because there just isn't enough room for all the cars to park. It seems as though everyone arrives at the same time.

We like our jelly stick because it's loaded with jelly and everything that's bad for us, and a nice cup of coffee that is always too hot. We get extra ice in a cup to help cool the coffee so we can eat and go on our way. On this day everyone was happy and in good spirits and when we left we said goodbye to our friends and headed for our favorite grocery store, Publix.

When we got to the store, I told George that I didn't have many things to buy so I wouldn't be very long inside the store. I told him that because he sometimes gets carried away talking to all his friends and eating samples the store gives away; he says it's his lunch.

I picked out a shopping cart that had a flat wheel that went thumping down each isle. It's customary to go around the store counterclockwise; I wonder who started that, we just do it. The last thing on my short list was WOW potato chips because Nancy likes them. When I got to where the chips were, I noticed there was only one large bag left and it was on the top shelf, almost out of reach. I had to be an acrobat to get it off the top shelf, but I got it down and into my shopping cart. You will notice that I'm making that plain.

On my way to the checkout cashier, I met the wife of a fellow airline worker whom I had known over the years. I rolled the cart around the corner and out of the way of other shoppers, and I talked to her for about five minutes. She told me that she had to go back to work teaching, because her husband's retirement benefits were being slashed and the airline was about to go bankrupt. When we were through talking, I turned to get my cart and it was gone. I looked down each aisle and could not find it. We laughed about it, but it wasn't funny, because in the cart was the last bag of WOW potato chips in the world.

I got another cart and retraced my steps to pick up the other four items on my list. Finally I got to the cashier and told her about it and she said it happens all the time. I guess I was looking for a little sympathy, but all I got was, *Who cares?*

I paid my small bill, and on my way out of the store, I walked past several other people being checked out, I usually look for other people that I know from Spruce Creek when I noticed a bag of WOW potato chips being put into a lady's bag. Then I noticed a double bag of Pringles, which was also in the cart I had. I stopped and looked in disbelief as she walked by me going to her car.

I couldn't help myself; I had to say something to George, who was walking alongside me, to tell him about the thief who had stolen my cart with WOW potato chips and a bag of Pringles. I said it loud enough for everyone in the vicinity to hear because I wanted to be heard. "George, what kind of a person would steal something from somebody else's cart, like WOW potato chips?" I casually looked in the direction of the chip-lifter and I heard her say to another lady, something about "that guy with the big mouth."

So ladies, the code is orange. Do not leave your purses unattended in a grocery store, a WOW potato chip thief is on the loose and will stop at nothing. We have since had a big laugh about all of this, but I at the time I gave her the benefit of the doubt because she was a big lady and could not have reached the top shelf anyway. My cart was also unattended, and she may have thought the items in there were for clerks to put back on the shelves. I really hope she enjoys those WOW potato chips. Choke, Choke!

A Genius

I have worked with a lot of mechanics over the years and believe me, there are all kinds. One in particular I want to tell you about exceeds every expectation known to man and if you were to see him work and complete jobs that seem impossible to you, you would see: He does the impossible.

I was driving to my hangar several days ago and came upon Steve, who was working on an old Dodge Omni. Steve has been a friend of mine for several years and his appearance is a wonder. He has a beard like Fidel; he wears his hair in a ponytail in the back, and generally, when you see him, he looks like he has been working for many hours without a break. Don't get me wrong: He works hard and knows what he is doing.

I wouldn't have given two cents for the car that he was working on, however, because the transmission was broken and the car would not go. After looking under the hood at the greasy mess that had held together for 185,000 miles, I thought to myself, *No way would I ever tackle anything like this*. He was going to fix it, though, because the owner had said that if Steve could get it running, he could have it.

The next day, I stopped by to see how he was doing. He had the front wheel off and was pounding on something under the fender. He was working on a bolt that held the cover on the transmission. The bolt, frozen from rust, was stuck hard and would not move. All the other bolts came out easily, but he was having trouble with that one. I would have thrown up my hands at that point, but not Steve. He just continued pounding on that bolt, because nothing seemed to bother him. He hooked up his electric drill and drilled the head off the bolt and then he was able to loosen the cover. Many taps with the hammer and chisel finally made all the parts come loose and off dropped the cover of the case to expose the gears inside. All the teeth on the gears were stripped. It looked impossible to fix. I would have thrown up my hands a second time and junked the car.

I saw Steve the next day, after he had been to a local junkyard. He had found a transmission from another car that wasn't even the same make or model, but he said, "That's all right. I think it'll fit because all the holes line up. It had better, because I paid $90 for it."

Still later, I stopped by again. He had the other transmission installed but did not have any controls hooked up, and had improvised a new gear shift lever, using different cables so it would shift gears.

I was a little bewildered by it all because he had no car to go back and forth to his house. I suspected he slept in the hangar each night. He said he would have this car running by that night, but in my mind, as I said, I would not have had it running by then or a year later.

Well, he didn't either. I stopped by after playing golf the next afternoon and he was just about ready to start the engine. I stood there when he pressed on the starter button, it turned over a few times but he had to choke it continually because it wouldn't run. It finally started, but sounded like a steam engine, going *fphit, fphit, fphit.*

As he moved around in front of the car, something blew his hat off. He turned off the engine and said that he had forgotten to put one of the spark plugs back into the engine, that's what blew his hat off. After looking around, he found a stray spark plug on the work bench. He proceeded to clean and gap it, even though it looked worn out, but he fixed it. He put in the plug and tightened it. When he started the engine the second time, it sounded like a smoothly running sewing machine.

To that point, he had not tried the gears in reverse or forward. For that matter, he had not even pushed on the clutch. As soon as he cleared all his tools away, he backed the car away from the building and took off down the roadway at 50 miles an hour. He came back the same way. When he pulled up in front of me, he jumped out of the car and said, "That transmission is too good for this car because it works like a charm."

The next day I decided to see how he was doing, and when I stopped by where he was working, I noticed the hood up again. A big compressor unit that runs the air conditioner was hanging out of the right side of the engine. In fact, there were other parts dangling here and there, and I asked what had happened.

He explained that, after all that work, he had decided to drive the car downtown to have something to eat. On the way, the engine blew a head gasket on two cylinders, so he drove the car back to the shop on the other two cylinders. It wouldn't go very fast but he made it back. By the time I got there, he had already put in a new head gasket, was putting all the loose parts back together and was just about ready to start it again.

Believe me, I had confidence in him. After all he had gone through up to now, I was sure it would run again. He pressed the starter button and it ran smoother than it did before. He adjusted the timing, added a little water to the radiator, and it sounded just fine. I think it's safe to say that he was ready to drive back to town again.

When he does, I hope he treats himself to a nice, big, thick, juicy steak for all his hard work. He surely deserves it. This man is my idea of a real mechanic: one who, when confronted with a situation, can figure out where the trouble lies and knows how to go about fixing it. With all the odds against him, he got that car running the way he said he would. They told him at the parts store that he was facing an impossible task. They didn't know Steve like I know him.

Now, that's genius.

SECTION FIVE:
TRAVEL TIDBITS

Into The West

The year following 2001, we slid gracefully through September 11th with no threats from terrorists. My wife and I decided to fly to Denver, Colorado, with Alma and Nick, who are Nancy's sister and her husband, to sightsee through the mountains. Alma's boss generously offered his villa for us to stay in. After a restful night's sleep, with bags packed and ready to go, thanks to Nancy, we loaded our luggage into the van of a friend, who had volunteered to get us to the airport on time. Away we went to Daytona Beach International Airport. After dropping our luggage curbside we went through more than the usual inspection of our carry-on baggage.

The inspector used a wand on every passenger to detect anything like metal and it seemed like an inconvenience but is very necessary. It is reassuring that the government is doing everything possible to prevent hijackers from getting on board aircraft. The inspector jokingly assured me that if he touched anything he wasn't supposed to, it would be purely accidental.

Our MD-80 took off a little late, which worried us because we had to make a connecting flight to Denver from Atlanta. As luck would have it, we landed in Atlanta on time, but still had to make a run for the other flight. The way the airport in Atlanta is laid out is not confusing but the long distances between planes makes one's heart beat a little faster.

The flight to Denver was fast and smooth: It couldn't have been any better. After landing, we stopped at the gate, but as we prepared to disembark there seemed to be a little confusion in the aisle. I guess with the excitement of getting there on time, people tend to get in a hurry to get their carry-on bags down from the rack. They know they can't move until the cabin door opens, but there are some who have a tendency to lean in that direction so there's bound to be a little pushing and shoving.

Nancy got up and was standing in the aisle to hold a space for me, so I jumped up and pulled my bag down from the rack. As we stood there people were starting to move. I noticed there was no one in front of the lady ahead of me. I had the luggage handle in my right hand behind me and my jacket in my left hand, ready to move. I heard the lady in front of me speak to someone who was seated and ask her if she wanted to go ahead of us. The lady said that she would rather wait, and for us to go ahead. When I heard that, I assumed the lady in front of me would start moving, when all of a sudden she turned around and started lashing out at me, yelling, "Don't be in such a rush." At first, I didn't think she was speaking to me because everyone in front of her had already left the cabin. She just stood there and would not move and was keeping everyone behind us from moving.

I assumed that we would then start moving, now that it had been established that the lady who was seated was not going ahead of us. Once again the lady in front of me turned around and lashed out at me, this time intimating that I had touched her. At that point I told her that I thought she was going to move because I was being pushed from behind and was trying to pull my carry-on bag behind me.

Another minute went by before she finally moved, and I told Nancy that she had accused me of putting my hands on her hips which was ridiculous because I had all I could do to move, with both hands full of luggage. She kept ranting and raving about what I had done to her and would not let up. After leaving the plane she went immediately to a telephone inside the terminal and as we walked by her, she said that her husband, whom she had called, had told her to sue me for assaulting her.

When we reached the carrousel she was still in a boxing match with herself. Alma, who had watched the entire goings-on, calmly walked over to a police officer who was standing nearby, just in case that crazy lady got violent. The police officer shook his head when he heard the lady say that she was going to sue me for assaulting her and that I should have apologized for touching her. The police officer kept shaking his head and said for us to go on our vacation and have a good time. We finally managed to find our luggage on the carousel and commandeered a porter to load it all onto a cart and take us to the bus that would transport us to the Avis Rent-a-Car lot.

Once on the bus we sighed with relief. With all that behind us, it should be clear sailing to get a van and drive off into the sunset. When we arrived at Avis, the bus driver drove all around to the other customers' cars and eventually got back to ours. We loaded the luggage into our rental van and once again drove off down the road, thinking all was well. With our entire luggage in the rear of the van, it's a wonder the front wheels didn't come off of the ground. If it had been an airplane, the nose wheel would have been unsteerable.

These problems didn't seem to bother Nick, Alma's husband who was driving. He carefully aimed the van down the road and on our way west. Nancy noticed that the back window on her side was open and the wind was threatening to blow her hat off. Nick pulled off the road and tried to close the window but realized that we needed assistance. We drove back to Avis to get help but could not find anyone who spoke English. After talking sign language to several people there, we got the window closed. I think rental companies should give a familiarization course on how to operate the doors and windows on new Dodge Vans. We were finally on our way once again, a little confused, but at least on the right road.

The ride to the villa took us through heavy traffic, but the wait was worth it. Alma's boss had a beautiful home in the mountains, with four bedrooms and five bathrooms on three floors. All the rooms are spacious and finished in natural wood. Our accommodations were absolutely perfect, and Henry had stocked the pantry and refrigerator with all kinds of food that made our stay delightful. The girls enjoyed going into the outside Jacuzzi, with the water temperature at 100 degrees and the outside air at 50 degrees.

The following day was a disappointment as it rained all day, but we were able to shop for more food and cuddle up that night on a luxurious lounge in front of the fireplace. I kept a list of all the places we went during the next eight days, and each one was more spectacular than the one before. We saw freshly-fallen snow on mountaintops, and we were at the Colorado River almost at its beginning near the top of the world. We crossed the continental divide three or four times at about the 13,000-foot level. From there we were able to see the river far below us, meandering at the bottom of the canyon, and it was simply breathtaking. I was glad to have on my Alaskan jacket with the hood pulled over my head that Nancy had so thoughtfully packed for just this occasion.

God did a good job in making this world and Noah did, too. We saw a total of about 75 elk in different herds, the largest of which was about 35; one had 17, another 10, some five or six. Some were so tame they were feeding on people's back lawns and sleeping in garden areas and in bushes. One large field had about 50 prairie dogs popping up from their holes in the ground.

This was our idea of a great vacation, and we got to see all kinds of animals in their own habitats which made us aware of our very fragile existence. It's a thrill to be on a mountaintop looking over this great land of ours.

On a much lighter note, when we stopped in town I went to the bookstores to tell them about my book. I found most of them receptive to the idea of a new book on the market and especially one about me. I also made a new friend who had just finished writing his own book, and with whom I made an even exchange.

Cruise To Panama

Nancy got four tickets to a fund raiser for Vince Carter, a famous basketball player who once played for the Toronto Raptors. We invited our dear friends, Les and Ann Lowman to go with us to the fund raiser because we seldom have the opportunity to share fun times together. When we presented our tickets at the door we were told to be sure to put our names and telephone numbers on the tickets. We had an enjoyable evening watching the auctioneer sell football helmets, basketballs, and all kinds of memorabilia from famous athletes.

The next morning, Nancy and I were seated at the breakfast table, going over some of the fun things that had gone on the night before, when the telephone rang. We looked each other, wondering who it could be. A lady's voice asked for David which brought a quizzical look on Nancy's face when she handed the phone to me. The voice belonged to Ann Smith who, after introducing herself, told me that she had good news for me. She said, "David, you have won the grand prize of a seven-day cruise in the Caribbean. Your ticket was drawn last night from all the ones that were at the fund raiser. Congratulations." Needless to say, when I repeated what she had just said, Nancy let out a scream of joy and I was still in shock. We thought it best to postpone the trip until after the first of the year and that is now.

The bus that was to take us to Fort Lauderdale arrived at Burger King on International Speedway at 5:00 a.m. Nancy and I boarded the bus while we watched Les start to drive my car back home. It all seemed like a dream at that time in the morning because I don't usually don't wake up until about seven. The bus ride was very fast and smooth and we beat all the traffic to Fort Lauderdale. Boarding the Princess is always a thrill. It's amazing how well the ship's captain and crew sail this big monstrosity of a vessel without bumping into something. We watched the departure from on deck and I wondered whether, if I were at the helm, I would run it aground.

We spent that day at sea and stopped at Key West for a shopping spree, and then we were on our way for the next two days. Seeing the Panama Canal for the first time and realizing the complex marvel of such an engineering feat really made us realize how lucky we were to enjoy this wonder and give our heartfelt gratitude for the workers who gave their lives for the sake of progress. They certainly did not then have the earth-moving capability that we have today, which would have shaved many months off the completion of this wonderful canal.

The technique of filling one chamber and emptying another at the same time and watching the different ships go up and down defies the imagination. After passing through the first locks we sat at anchor for about two hours and came back out the way we came in, all the time watching our progress on the TV monitor. It is something that everyone should do once in a lifetime.

We stopped at Grand Cayman Island where Nancy took a little side trip with a boatload of people who like to snorkel. She swam with stingrays and all kinds of fish while I went shopping on shore. We stopped at Cozumel to see the ruins, and naturally Nancy climbed the 100 steps up to the highest point and took fantastic pictures from the top. We are getting the urge to go again, I know not where: Nancy will know!

How Easy It Would Be

It was one of those beautiful mornings: no clouds in the sky, a slight breeze, and sunny. It was the third day of our yearly vacation in south Florida at a timeshare unit that overlooks the ocean. I had just finished washing the dishes after cooking one of my gourmet omelets for Nancy. She was standing outside on the balcony, overlooking Jensen Beach, when she noticed a small plane flying quite low over a residential area. The condos and buildings to the south of us partially obscured the plane as it passed low and out of sight.

At first she didn't think it too unusual for the plane to be that low, because we both fly and we live in a community where lots of planes fly in the area. But Federal Air Regulations state that aircraft are not allowed to fly below 1,000 feet over heavily populated areas. As Nancy hung over the balcony to see what the pilot was going to do next, he swooped down to treetop level and appeared to be buzzing someone on the ground, as some do—which is absolutely against the law. Then she realized that I should be watching too, because she knows how excited I get when planes appear to be in trouble or when some kooky pilot decides to do something crazy like this.

She called for me to come out and look because it could become a dangerous situation. I, too, was surprised to see how low this joker was flying over a populated area and the questions were running rampant in my head, as to what his intention was. Then I noticed, on one of his passes at treetop level, that it was an aggie plane, used mostly to spray insecticides and fertilizer over farm land. But what was he spraying in this area, surrounded by so many hotels on the beaches? As quickly as he had appeared, he disappeared to the north by flying up the river at a very low altitude.

Nancy decided to get our binoculars and take a closer look in that direction from the end of the building. Then the scare of our life came with what we saw through the lens, and it gave us both chills. We were looking at the Saint Lucie power plant, which is about 15 miles to the north, and the plane appeared to be swooping down over the buildings. We were terrified that if he were a terrorist and had stolen that plane and had plans to blow up the power plant, we could do nothing about it.

There was no other plane or helicopter in the vicinity and if the pilot were in fact a terrorist, we would both be dead along with hundreds of thousands of other people. As a precaution, Nancy called 911. The operator said she knew nothing about a low flying plane over the area and that there had been no other reports about it.

We both mulled over in our minds the possibility that this particular situation could be a wake-up call to avoid a future disaster, but again decided there was nothing more we could do. We watched the plane through the binoculars for a little while longer until it finally disappeared behind the buildings. Thank heavens that nothing happened. He must have been spraying for mosquitoes after all. We walked back inside our apartment, sighed in relief, glad to be alive. We wondered if that was the way it was going to be from now on.

I guess when things like this occur we must use good judgment and basic common sense to keep from flipping out and causing a disaster from our imagination.

We spent the next seven days going out to dinner, seeing a couple of good movies and going to a nice baseball game. The guys who play in the minor leagues really play hard, and we saw four home runs in that game. It is such a pleasure to be at the games in person, because at all of the baseball stadiums the field is manicured and you hear sounds you ordinarily don't hear on TV, like the crack of the bat hitting the ball and the remarks yelled from the grandstand. People get pretty excited when the umpire calls what the audience thinks should be the opposite of what he called.

We went on a boat ride to Jupiter lighthouse, just north of Palm Beach. We were served a nice lunch and we even saw two dolphins having fun in their playful way, diving under the bow of our boat as if leading us on our way. On another ride we took a smaller, local pontoon boat that wound in and around the mangroves, so that we could see critters along the shore.

Nancy was up at the crack of dawn every morning, walking the beach, and much to her surprise the sand dunes were all flattened down from high winds and high tides during the recent hurricanes and from all the storms we have had this past two years.

Somehow our week's vacations seem to be getting shorter each year. We find more interesting things to do that we enjoy doing together. But this time, a tropical storm was down in the straits and coming our way so we had to cut short the last day of our vacation and head for home early on Sunday morning.

It is always fun to go away on a vacation, after working hard at what you do, day after day. But it is also nice to come home and sleep in your own bed.

Mmmmm. Zzzzzzzz.

A Sharp Knife

As many times as I have had to slice tomatoes, I am ever so thankful that I have a sharp knife to do the job. I have one particular knife that slices right through the outer skins and I figure that there is no other one in the whole world that can do it better. I never thought I would put our tomato-cutting knife up to a challenge against an unknown brand!

We go on vacation every year at the same time because we have a timeshare in Stuart, Florida. It's a condo on Hutchinson Island that our family has owned for over 30 years. Every year when we go there, we find that the condo association has done something to improve our apartment. This year they installed new sliding doors which work with delightful smoothness. They also added new pots and pans, silverware, and one knife. I'm not in the habit of getting excited about a new knife and I didn't think much about it until the following morning.

You see, I am still cooking breakfast for the two of us, Nancy and myself, because I make eggs the way we like them and it is something I enjoy doing, even on vacation. So I picked the new knife out of the drawer, scientifically held it over a fresh tomato as if I were going to perform a vasectomy on it, and proceeded to slice. With one fell swoop I pressed and sliced through the tomato as if it were butter. I was astonished that it did so well and I had to admit my own first place, award-winning knife slid into second place and it was no compromise on my part. The votes were in: This knife won hands down.

I don't know why I'm making such a big deal about this knife, because it wasn't the most important thing that I wanted to talk about, but anyway, I had to have a knife like that. That morning after breakfast we passed by the office on our way out shopping. I asked the lady behind the desk if, by any chance, they had any extra knives that I could buy. She informed us that generally, the association buys an assortment of silverware and they seldom have extras for sale. We started to leave and the assistant housekeeper Roseanne followed us out the door and asked to see the knife. We took her back upstairs to our apartment and showed her the knife. She asked to borrow it and said that she would be right back. She came back in ten minutes with another knife like the one we had shown her and said we could have it.

Not wanting something for nothing, I offered her money which she said she could not accept. I immediately went downstairs to my car and brought one of my books and gave it to her for going to all that trouble. You might have thought I had given her a million dollars because the first thing out of her mouth after she read the title, *Memoirs of a Little Italian Boy*, was that she also was Italian. She raved about it and then declared that her whole family in New York would buy copies, without her even having read it.

We parted company and we didn't see her until the morning we left. She said she was halfway through reading the book and wanted me to sign it. She was thrilled to have met us again before we left. My book seems to have led me into new friendships that I would not have otherwise made.

The Little Italian Boy is at it again, making new readers and friends.

Flight From Frances

Hurricane Francis started off the coast of Africa as a mild-mannered tropical storm. As it strengthened, it became a challenge to all the weather channels, trying to predict where it would end up. But somehow this one had its sights on Florida long before anyone else knew where it was going.

Most everyone stayed busy in their daily routines while Francis churned a little faster and grew a little bigger each day. I have learned during my years in Florida to keep a weary eye on these devils, not to get too excited about their coming, but to keep watching with one eye and make preparations, in case of their arrival.

Luckily, Nancy thinks much farther ahead than most of us, and she starts at a casual pace putting together all the items we will need if we have to make a run for it. When the weather stations notify us that this one is coming straight for us and to take the necessary safety precautions, we know it's time to move. I made a quick decision to cover our two front windows and the three small windows in our den, which worked out pretty well. That was all I had time for.

Nancy had called ahead to Hampton Inn in Tifton, Georgia four days before and had been able to get reservations for us and the two dogs, with an adjacent room for her mom.

Thursday morning at 3:00 a.m. we all hit the deck running. While I cooked breakfast, Nancy got both cars packed, her mom dressed, and breakfast ready on the table. After eating and washing dishes, we were out the door at 4:00, power and water turned off. Several times this past hurricane season, we had decided to outrun the storms by heading north to higher and safer ground. Our decision to leave at four o'clock in the morning was the right one because the traffic frenzy had not yet begun. The people who leave later are caught in much more traffic than we are.

Our two cars left the front gate at five minutes past the hour. We went the back way to DeLand, with Nancy leading over the bumpy road to Route 40. We sailed right along, took the cutoff on 326 to I-75 and we were in Tifton in exactly five hours.

The ride from Daytona Beach to the outskirts of Ocala was uneventful because of the hour. After a 15-minute stop to get a Coke and let our two dogs irrigate the gas station lawn, we were on our way north on I-75. There was a definite change in attitude and speed the minute we merged into this super racetrack. We blended into traffic nicely and I set 70 on the cruise control.

Then I started to watch for drivers in front of us who might be going slower because I didn't want to slam into someone driving 60 or 65 m.p.h. Did I say slower? I have to rethink what I just said, because that was a joke. There was nobody going as slow as 65. In fact, several drivers came up close behind us and blinked their lights or continued around us. Not wanting to create a bottleneck, I turned off the cruise control and sped up to 75 m.p.h. That speed seemed alright for a while until daylight began to brighten the sky and then it became a free-for-all.

Trucks and cars surrounded us and to keep someone from running into us, I started cruising at 80. Semi-trucks were still passing us and they had to be doing 85 or 90 m.p.h. and that's a fact. I just don't like to be in a situation going that fast and have no place to go in an emergency: It is just plain dumb. I had to slow down and let everyone go past me, or speed up and get ahead of everyone. The latter is extremely dangerous. I have found it's best to pull off at the nearest exit and have a Coke and stretch my legs.

We had beat the heavy traffic by two hours because not long after we were settled in our motel room, we could see the traffic had started to back up and it stayed that way for the rest of the day. The steady roar of diesel trucks and car engines shifting gears filled the air. We heard sirens from ambulances and police cars all night, but we were tired enough to sleep with all that noise.

We had three wonderful days of sunshine and good weather, and then the rains came. Our motel rooms were on the second floor facing the pool, while the other rooms faced the parking lot. When they built the motel they made space behind all of our rooms, from one end to the other, on both floors, for boilers, laundry and storage. During the heaviest rainstorm, the rain spout from the roof that connects to another spout behind our room came loose and was flooding the whole area behind us. I got up about midnight and walked barefoot into the bathroom and was up to my ankles in water. When I turned on the light, Nancy woke up and we both tried to mop faster than the water coming in. We called for help and they came with big towels which helped until the janitor got the pipe hooked up again. It was too late because the water had already reached the rug ten feet into the room.

We slept there for the night but in the morning we had to change rooms, so back to packing and moving everything. We found out later that eight rooms were flooded but none as badly as ours.

The one good thing about this Hampton Inn was that they provided breakfast every morning: juice, fruit, eggs, cereal, coffee and donuts. Best of all we had our dogs with us and they were wonderful traveling companions. The dogs took on a different personality because they seemed to be enjoying the new goings-on. They had to go up and down stairs to do their business and it gave them a chance to see a new outside world, some place different than their backyard.

For dinner we went to Appleby's, which was just around the corner. Everything was close by, like K-Mart and Wal-Mart etc; so it kept travel to a minimum because gasoline was getting harder to get. We were there about six days until after the storm had passed.

We came back the following Wednesday, straight through again in five hours and so glad to be back home, with minimal damage and that only to trees. The biggest mess was in the pool: It was filled with about ten bushels of leaves and small branches. It took about five days to get it clean again.

My Trip To Boise

In 1977, I flew from Miami to Boise to see John Henrickson, a man with whom I had worked as a mechanic at Eastern Airlines. John had gone through a divorce in Miami and was in Boise where his mom and dad still were living. His dad was 92 years young and still scratching in the garden, growing things like he had done all of his life. I was astonished to see how easily he was moving around in the middle of his vegetable garden, using the rake and hoe.

John met me at Boise airport when I flew in from Sun River. I had the use of Bill Walter's Aerostar, the plane that I had been flying and maintaining for the past five years. I decided this was going to be the last opportunity I would have to fly it.

That night John drove me to an area where they were spraying insecticides from helicopters, a night-time spraying which I had never seen before. They were not able to spray in the daytime for fear of killing honey bees that were pollinating.

The following day we took off in the Aerostar to see beautiful, mountainous country to the north. It was only a 30-minute ride to McCall, but going there we passed over Lake Cascade about 15 miles before landing at McCall, which holds the Payette Lakes: beautiful country. We had a jitney car, a 57 Chevy lent to us by the FBO at the airport, and we drove up to a fire lookout station. The people there were friendly and told us all about their duties as fire lookouts in a very dangerous, wooded area. I remember flying over Lake Lowell when I flew John back to Nampa. I then had to go to Sun River, where Bill and his wife Lucy had bought a new home. Then I had to hightail it back to Miami the next morning on Eastern.

San Diego

We planned to take our 1997 summer vacation after a workshop that Nancy had attended earlier in the week in San Diego, California. I flew out and met her in the airline terminal on Saturday. We rented a car and were on our way almost before we said, *hello*. But that's the way we do things, fast and furious.

We headed for Yuma, Arizona, hoping to see some exciting new landscapes. Our speedometer needle was bouncing on 75 miles per hour and the road ahead was clear. The first part of the trip, which was mostly in California, we saw date trees growing and not much else. I'll bet most of you never even stopped to wonder if dates grow on bushes or on trees. We stopped to have lunch in a little town out in the middle of nowhere. I had a milkshake made with fresh dates which had an unusual taste that I had never tried before. It was the only flavor they had and I guess if they grew figs or bananas they would have put those into it, too.

We continued down the road through complete desolation. There was absolutely nothing to look at on either side of the road. It was not a very good place to run out of gas or have car trouble.

After crossing the Arizona state line, we stopped at a gas station in Yuma. It reminded me of my home town when I was a kid, when on a Sunday afternoon all the stores were closed and people went for rides in the country. It was a déjà vu experience.

While Nancy went into the gas station to buy a Coke, I looked around and could see no one, so I sat for a moment looking across the street. There was a dilapidated-looking fence around a little old house where someone apparently lived. It was evidenced by a few redundant toys in the front yard that had outlived their usefulness. The fence reminded me of one I might, as a kid, have leaned against or rattled a stick across in a devilish gesture to irritate the owner of the house. The houses in the area looked a lot alike and they seemed very quiet, as if everyone had left town for the day.

There were no gangs of kids screaming and yelling or playing ball, except for two who suddenly rode up on their bikes to buy Cokes. It didn't seem like these country folks had very much to do and were just staying out of sight. The day was sunny and hot and it was just a quiet Sunday afternoon, the way Sundays used to be when I was a kid: just another lazy day in this little town.

We spent the night in Yuma and the following nights in Phoenix and then Sun Mesa, then the next three nights in Sedona. Without a doubt Sedona is one of the most beautiful towns we have ever seen. The motel was on the main road through town and the back porch of our unit faced east, toward the mountains. The sun coming up over the mountains in the morning, shining on same mountains at sunset, was really breathtaking.

We were within walking distance of a little Italian restaurant around the corner that made the most delicious pasta dishes we ever had. The wine added just enough pleasure to make each mealtime a honeymoon extravaganza. Having the motel close by made the last little swig of wine that much more enjoyable. We watched the sunsets from our balcony and enjoyed the changing colors against the red mountains.

The next day we took a Jeep ride to a place we had heard much about, called Boynton Canyon Vortex. I understood very little of what we were about to see and do. Besides the driver we were the only ones in the rickety old Jeep. The ride was no less impressive than if we had been put in a salt shaker then dashed up and down several times, finally being sprinkled on a great big, juicy steak. I think there were times Nancy and I questioned our decision to take this crazy ride with a complete stranger. He looked like someone you might find at the entrance to a super highway holding a sign that said, "Will work for food." Our insides fortunately did not succumb to all the jostling around, but when we finally came to a full stop we were still jiggling.

We walked from the Jeep down a path leading to a grassy, tree-covered area, and just beyond it we came to a slow-flowing stream. We walked to the water's edge and there our guide related a story about the stream. It flowed lazily over flat rocks where Indians were said to have held ceremonial prayers for girls who had just become women and had become fertile. It wasn't quite clear what they did but I supposed they might have submerged them. It was explained to us as a very sacred place, but I got no vibes there. It seemed magical but was only a part of the beautiful mountain scenery basking in the sun's glow.

We drove to a different area, higher in another part of the Mesa, close by. It was another bone-bouncing, flesh-jiggling, mind-boggling ride. We left the Jeep and walked up a rocky path to a place near the top of the mountain. There we stood in a clearing, overlooking a deep and wide, green valley of bushes and trees, stretching toward more mountains, many miles away, that formed a big amphitheater.

Of all the places on Earth one might expect Christ might come back to, this place seemed worthy of his presence—it was so beautiful. The only other time I had a similar feeling was in St. Peter's Church in Italy. For just a moment, it was as if we were standing at a point where two magnetic lines met and the feeling was so powerful it is indescribable. At that moment I became emotionally strengthened and overwhelmed with such joy.

I guess we never forget where we came from in our childhood. My family didn't have much, and certainly none of the luxury that we see in our daily living today. Things were simple. We had a lot of fun going to movies on Sunday afternoons or taking quiet walks on the beach. We started our lives quite simply but the world has evolved into a state of advanced technology to a point where we have lost sight of reality. Kids can do things on skateboards, bicycles, and motorbikes that were not even thought of in the early part of the 20th century. Men have been on the moon, and are thinking about going to the planet Mars, so I guess anything is possible.

SECTION SIX: REFLECTIONS

A Different Time

In the late 1950s, when the new DC-8s arrived from the factory, it was the most exciting thing to happen in aviation for a long time, not only because the planes were sparkling new but because they were jets, entirely different from propeller type airplanes. It was strange not to see a propeller out in front of an engine and to see the jet engines hanging below the wings instead of on them. To this airline mechanic, this was a new concept in design and operation, something I got used to only after studying operation manuals.

One big, particularly obvious difference was the sweptback wings on either side that appeared to be more streamlined, which made jet planes capable of flying higher and faster and carrying more people and baggage because the engines had more power.

On one of my first trips from Boston to Miami in a new jet, I had a window seat and I could see the whole city of New York as we climbed to 35,000 feet. It was magnificent because it had snowed the night before.

The Captain announced that passengers on the right side of the cabin could see the city. It was nine o'clock in the morning, the sun was shining brightly, and those who were able were looking down at this sight. I thought to myself, *There must be ten million people down there, and each one of them thinks that he or she has got the biggest problem in the whole world.* My very next thought was, *I can't even see those people down there; much less their problems.*

Today, September 11, 2001, their problems have been shown to me. It has been 43 years since my first sight of the city was indelibly etched in my mind. I expect that if I live another 43 years the sight of the two burning towers will still be imprinted as clearly as it is this day.

War And Remembrance

The front page of *USA Weekend Magazine* for May 21 2001, showed news anchor Tom Brokaw and actor Ben Affleck, who starred in the recently released film, *Pearl Harbor*. They were standing next to a Navy plane, possibly an F6F, on the deck of the *USS Intrepid*, an aircraft carrier now docked as a museum on the Hudson River in New York City. More than 200 *Intrepid* crewmen died in World War II, half of them when the ship was hit by kamikaze pilots.

For their two hours together, both the TV anchor and the actor seemed to sense that the ship was a sacred place. Brokaw asked Affleck, "Before this project, did you think about the war much?"

Affleck's reply was, "Not really. It was a distant, abstract time seen in black-and-white pictures."

To me it was a perfect summary, one that I totally understood. But that wasn't my experience, because in 1941 I was just out of high school and working as an aircraft mechanic at my hometown airport in Beverly, MA. On that particular Sunday I was called into work because the regular man was out sick.

When the news came over the radio, the broadcast was about the Japanese bombing Pearl Harbor. We didn't realize the severity of the damage to our naval fleet until the next day, when President Roosevelt gave the speech that became so famous over time, about the dastardly attack by the Japanese. Unfortunately, we did not have television to show us the damage that was done.

I went to all of the recruiting stations the next day to see if I could get into Navy or Army aviation. No one could guarantee I would not end up in the walking Army or as a seaman in the Navy. Everything was in complete confusion, and no one knew exactly what to do, so I decided to wait. When things calmed down, I enlisted in the Navy and stayed on inactive duty, because I worked for a company that had a contract with the Navy to train cadets how to fly; called the V5 program. Later, I went on active duty as a Machinist Mate Third Class, during which time I repaired TBF Torpedo Bombers, some of which had seen action.

Getting back to Ben Affleck, when he said the war was a distant abstract: I can understand why he felt that way about Pearl Harbor, because for someone who was not old enough to be in the war, it does seem distant. I felt the same way about World War I, because that took place before I was born. Even though it seems distant we should never forget how lucky we are to be still living under an American flag, and not a Japanese or German one. If, after they bombed Pearl Harbor, the Japanese had planned a landing on the United States and were able to successfully carry it through, there is no telling what might have happened.

It may seem like 60 years was a long time ago, but let me tell you, snap your fingers a couple of times and another 60 years will have gone by. At times, I feel that the younger generation does not really understand or appreciate how lucky they are to be Americans in America. They seem not to be thankful for all that the men and women during WWII and subsequent wars did for them, especially those who fought and gave their lives so that we could all live free.

I gave more than three years of my life to the Navy and I wouldn't hesitate to give more if I had to. I'm probably too old now, but just maybe, if they could find some place for me to fit into, like the cockpit of an old F6F or a P51 Mustang . . .

Brokaw summed it up quite nicely when he said that when people came back from the war, they were desperate to put it behind them and didn't want to talk about it anymore. Now they are in a mortality zone. They are looking back and saying, *Whatever else I did in my life, I did that. I had a part in something that was larger than our ability to understand it.*

Young people, you are free today because of the many who gave their lives.

Good Deed For The Day

One day on the way home from the hangar I keep my plane in, I noticed a biplane taxiing toward the runway. At the controls was my friend, Lenny in his 1941 Waco biplane. As he taxied near the tree where pilots sometimes stop to chat, and have a smoke to relax, he swung the plane around and shut it off. When I walked toward his plane, I could see he had a passenger in the front cockpit. I asked him how the flight was and he informed me that they hadn't been flying, that it was just an indoctrination, a taxiing exercise to get the passenger, a lady, used to being inside the plane.

When she got out and walked down over the wing, she explained that she had a problem being in enclosed areas, due to claustrophobia. She thought that by being in an open cockpit with nothing but a wing over her head she would be able to overcome this problem. Lenny asked me to accompany her on her first flight in that plane, but she still did not want to do it.

I invited her to walk with me to a bench under the tree and sit a moment while I explained to her how safe she would be in the plane, that he was a safe pilot, and to encourage her to relax and go with the flow. I finally convinced her to walk back to the plane with me. When I helped her get up onto the wing, she turned and said that if I would go, then she would go, too. I agreed, just to make sure she didn't back down.

We both squeezed into the front cockpit, and we got our safety belts on and the little side door closed. When Lenny started the engine, she grabbed my hands as if to reassure herself that I wasn't going to jump out and leave her. As we taxied toward the runway, she became very nervous: She almost pulled my thumb out of its socket. I kept telling her to be calm, and shook her hands to make her relax. It worked fine until we started down the runway. When the plane lifted off she was hanging on to me for dear life. I shook her hands again and it seemed to remind her to relax. When we climbed a little higher and made the first turn downwind the same thing happened: She really tensed up and closed her eyes. I reassured her that everything was still all right but that it was going to be necessary to make another turn, making one wing dip down, so that we could get back to the airport. Every time the plane did anything besides go straight ahead she was in a panic.

When we turned onto final approach, Lenny cut the engine and I thought the lady was going to jump out, but I was able to convince her it was the only way to land the plane. The plane lurched a little when we landed, which is normal, and she grabbed me one more time and then relaxed.

When we taxied back to the tree she started shouting, "I did it!" She was so proud of her accomplishment and, after thanking Lenny for the ride, left to tell her husband about it, extremely happy that it was all over.

I have taken up several people who were petrified for one reason or another. I have found that if I talk to them in a calming manner beforehand, it helps to reassure them that everything will be all right.

One frightened fellow I took up for the first time actually turned green, but he didn't get sick. He was so proud of himself that he asked if I would take him up again. That time he looked—well, glanced—out of the window. When we turned on final, he asked "Are we down yet?" That incident was a big accomplishment for me because my brother had been trying unsuccessfully to take the man up for years.

Some people are afraid of flying because they do not understand what makes an airplane fly. In a nutshell, this is why and how an airplane is able to fly. An airplane has an engine for power and when the engine starts, it turns a propeller, usually in the front, which pulls the airplane through the air. The faster an engine runs, the quicker the propeller turns, which in turn pulls the plane fast enough through the air for the wings to have lift.

Because a wing is curved on top and flat on the bottom, a molecule of air that passes over the top of the wing travels further to reach the trailing edge than a molecule passing under the wing. The faster air over the top creates a vacuum, or lift, as it is called, and the air under the flat wing on most planes produces pressure on the bottom of the wing, thereby lifting the plane off the ground.

At the same time, the tail plays three important roles. First, elevators mounted onto a horizontal stabilizer guide the nose of the plane in an up-and-down movement that governs the speed. While in flight the elevator is moved when the control stick or wheel is pulled back gently. This makes the nose go up, which slows the airplane to a lower speed as it struggles to go up. If the control stick is pushed forward gently, the nose goes down and the plane picks up speed.

The rudder also controls yaw, meaning the nose will turn left or right when needed. It controls skidding and slipping in a turn. If you apply too much rudder in a turn, you will skid the same way you would if, in a car, if you turned the wheel too hard on a slippery road. If you apply too little rudder then you will slip around the turn.

The third function is the vertical stabilizer, which is set and does not move. Most people do not realize how important this function is. It keeps the airplane stable, helps overcome torque from the engine in straight and level flight and is a necessary place to hang the rudder.

The last and most important thing that helps an airplane to fly is a competent person at the controls who has to be qualified and licensed. I have found that flying is the most exhilarating thing that I have accomplished in my lifetime of dreams. Most people who are able to drive a car can learn to fly if they so desire. But I'm glad that some of the people, who drive, do not fly.

Boom! Boom!

I was awakened from a light sleep in the early morning hours by two sonic booms. Our two dogs heard them too, and they let us know they had. It's almost as if the dogs had left a wake-up call with NASA and asked that the shuttle come overhead at 4:57 a.m. and make two sonic booms, so that Mom would wake up, too. Then the dogs could sit with her while she read a few paragraphs in her book. She likes to have them with her too, so she can feel fur. This seems to start her day in a tranquil mood.

Somehow it doesn't seem real that NASA had men circling the earth for 10 days. They repaired the Hubble telescope and returned safely to Earth. To bring the shuttle back, it must slice into the earth's atmosphere at the proper angle or it might bounce off and slip back into space.

On one of the last orbits before re-entering the atmosphere, the crew prepares the shuttle for landing by securing everything inside the ship. They are securely fastened in their seats and have pressure suits on in preparation for re-entry and landing. With all things secured, the ship must be maneuvered so that it is going backwards; it is upside down facing the earth. Before firing the retro rockets the ship is in a nine-and-three position: tail towards the nine on a clock, the nose towards the three, belly pointing skyward. Then it is repositioned to an approximate eight-and-two position, tail at eight and nose at two, which is a predetermined down angle in preparation for retro firing. Then the retro rockets are fired for a brief period to slow the ship from its 17,000 mile-an-hour race through space. This usually takes place between Madagascar and Australia.

After the retro rockets finish burnout, the ship must turn its nose up away from Earth and continue to come around until the nose is pointing to eleven and tail to five o'clock. In this nose-high entry position, the bottom of the fuselage, which is covered with the heat shield tiles, is ready for the entry interface. Then comes the fiery entrance into the earth's atmosphere which is very critical and must be done precisely.

Once the flaming shuttle has entered the earth's atmosphere and the fire is out and it has slowed it down, the pilot has control and begins to fly it. The slowing-down process and many maneuvers that the pilot has to make call for all the knowledge the pilot has learned in his training because he has a tiger by the tail.

The shuttle comes over the Kennedy Space Center in Florida at about 10,000 feet, still traveling about 1,000 m.p.h. Then the familiar sonic booms are heard to announce its arrival, and then the pilot guides it to a safe landing as it comes over the threshold, still barreling along at more than 200 m.p.h.

I remember as a young boy, long before television, listening to radio programs like *Buck Rogers in the 25th Century*. We used a lot of imagination and in our minds we focused 500 years into the future. We thought the man who conceived Buck Rogers' character was either nuts or way ahead of his time. What I imagined then has already come true, and it's only the 21st century. We now send manned rockets into orbit and we have men outside their craft performing duties hundreds of miles above the earth.

We have sent men to the moon, safely landed them there and then brought them home. It shows that we almost have the capability to go to other planets and land and come back safely. Whoever does that may have to give his life up to the program with the possibility of no return. Unless scientists find a faster way to travel through space, it might take too long to go to the planet Mars and return. We will have to wait and see.

I also remember Dick Tracy and his radio wristwatch, which was a radio telephone too. It seemed farfetched at the time, but it's here now. It seems like nothing is beyond man's imagination. Physicians take out old, broken-down parts from our bodies and replace them with new parts from other people. They can also manufacture parts like new hip and knee joints. After the replacement, the person is walking in a few days' time.

We live in an age of wonder, and exciting new things are happening all the time. We put this inanimate object (the computer) to work and find somebody we haven't seen or talked to in years and can be talking to them in seconds. We go online and purchase our own airline tickets to anywhere in the world and never talk to an agent. We take a picture of a loved one and send it to another family member in seconds.

Are we going too fast? I don't think so. The thing we must remember is that we have to make each day count for something, no matter how small or insignificant it seems. The one thing we must not forget through all of this is to be kind to each other. We all have the right and privilege to live in peace with each other on this beautiful earth.

Bronchitis And Bike Week

I was all prepped and ready when they wheeled me into the operating room, where I was to get a bronchoscopy examination. I was clearheaded as much as I ever am, lying there looking up at the ceiling. The time was just five minutes to eleven and the procedure was scheduled for eleven. I couldn't understand why no one was paying attention to me. A male nurse started to push me back to the room and I asked her, "When are they going to start? "

He said, "You're already done."

I could not believe my ears and thought someone had stolen my brain. I would like to see what actually takes place behind the scenes. Imagine a doctor and a nurse standing behind a one-way window. The doctor gives a signal to the anesthesiologist who turns on the juice and the patient disappears.

They crammed the tube down my throat and looked around inside my lung and sloshed some saline solution all around and did what ever they had to do, which took about 30 minutes. Then attendant took all the evidence away and hid it and the doctor went on his merry way. In the meantime enough time had gone by for my body to reappear in the next scene, which took place when they pushed me back to the room.

I could not have felt better than I did right then because I had a certain amount of fear going in and that was totally unfounded. This all goes back to the previous Sunday night, when we'd had a delightful dinner at a local restaurant and come away happy and satisfied. As the evening progressed and we had made ourselves comfortable watching TV, I had noticed a different feeling come over me. I'd sat up and taken notice of this strangeness making me feel like I was becoming disconnected. I had felt this many times before and knew right what to do.

I immediately undressed and went to bed and asked my wife Nancy to make a pot of hot tea and get my antibiotic pills because I was starting to shake all over. I got through the night with high fever and severe shakes, on the verge of pneumonia. We went to see the doctor the next day and he put me into the hospital. I went through a series of tests until the following Friday, when I had the above procedure done and then I was sent home.

I did want to tell about the person in the next bed to me. It was bike week and he had been in an accident while riding his motorcycle north on Ridgewood Ave. A lady who was driving south in her car decided to make a left turn right in front of him and slam on her brakes. He crashed into the side of her car, and he and his wife, who was riding on the back of his cycle, went flying over the handlebars and over the car on to the median. His wife landed about twenty feet from him and she suffered a broken ankle and foot and he had multiple injuries: broken knee, leg, ribs, shoulder and collar bone and I don't know what all else but he was in bad shape, Lucky he was only doing 35 m.p.h. or he might have been killed.

With this one accident I must come to his defense. It was all because of a negligent driver who did not give way to oncoming traffic, which has been a steadfast rule of the road ever since I have been driving and that has been over 70 years. Unfortunately we have become a nation of fast-driving maniacs and when we get that power in our hands we become kings and queens of the road. All we have to do is ask that lady if she feels like a queen.

A New Heart Start

There is nothing that is absolute or for sure in this world in regard to health or life. We are here for just a short time and it is a sin to waste one minute of that time, and that is why I'm writing this portion of my life.

I thought, because I had two brothers who were 95 and 93 years old and a sister who was 87, that my genes were good and I had plenty of years to go. I am now 84 and I have done just about everything that I wanted to, so why should I worry about anything, especially my health? I had noticed at times over the past two years that I had shortness of breath, especially after pulling the plane out of the hangar. I thought it was old age creeping up on me, but I didn't want to admit it to myself. I had never taken a stress test, because I never saw the need and I wasn't really looking for trouble. I hope what I am about to tell you scares you enough to go to a doctor, if you do have shortness of breath, to have a stress test done. It might be nothing to worry about, but why take a chance? Let the doctor decide what else should be done.

Monday, October 20, 2003 my wife, Nancy and I were sitting in the den. She was at the computer and I was watching the boob tube. Believe me it scares me to tell about it now. I started to get a mild pain in my chest, right in the middle, as if I had indigestion. I didn't panic but I did say, "Honey, come sit with me," because I had a strange feeling that it was more than indigestion. I told her that I felt normal everywhere else and I didn't think it was my heart. Wasn't it stupid for me to diagnose myself, because I had no idea what a heart attack felt like? She jokingly said, "You are not leaving me" and the pain went away.

I slept well that night, then got up the next morning and made breakfast for the both of us and went back to bed for a snooze, a habit I have gotten into this past few years, which I think is another signal that something is wrong. After the snooze I got dressed and picked up George, my father in-law. We started on our daily excursion to the donut shop, Madison's, on Ridgewood Avenue. We have been going there since Dunkin' Donuts closed three of their stores and we found that Madison's donuts were better, especially their jelly sticks, which look like crullers but are filled with jelly that oozes out all over the place.

Then we stopped for a short visit at Publix and were back home by early afternoon. It was time to cut my lawn, so I got my rider mower's tires pumped up to the proper pressure, filled the gas tank and buzzed around the back yard and got that done in a half hour, empted the three buckets of leaves and grass down over the hill and then drove out to the front yard and finished mowing the front swale, at which time I usually empty the big buckets and then proceed to finish the lawn.

I went to the side of the house where I empty the buckets down over the banking. On my way up the hill that same pain I had the night before hit me right in the middle of my chest and I knew that something was definitely wrong. I struggled to the top of the hill and set the bucket down, then walked very carefully to my kitchen and picked up the phone to call Les, who is a partner in our airplane. His wife, Ann answered and told me he was at work somewhere in Spruce Creek. I asked Ann to hurry over to my house because I was having chest pains. She arrived two minutes later, saw the condition I was in and called Ann Adams, whom she knew was a nurse. I was sitting in the back of my station wagon while I waited, sweating pretty heavily, and then I started to sweat even more. Ann came a few minutes later, took my blood pressure and said we had better get to the hospital. I hardly remember insisting on taking a shower, but I did because I didn't want to end up dirty in the emergency room.

We got into her big, beautiful Lincoln SUV and sped off the hospital. I remember telling them to call my wife, Nancy, who met us at the door, where they took me right in. I don't remember how long I was in emergency; it seemed like a long time. The next day they tried to do a catheterization of the heart to see if they could open up any arteries. This proved futile because everything was blocked.

The following day, Thursday, they performed open-heart surgery on me and did five bypasses. I did not feel a thing or have any pain during the operation. I'm amazed because it seems like a miracle has been performed on me. The only discomfort after the operation was that I have to lie on my back, which makes sleeping difficult.

I can't say enough about the nurses, both men and women, who cared for me. They did an outstanding job, and the hospital went out of its way to make me comfortable and keep me happy. When they wheeled me out of the hospital to Nancy's car all I could think of was to sing, *Goodbye Forever* to all the nurses as I passed by their stations.

I have been home now with Nancy caring for me and am feeling wonderful. The weather has been terrible the last few days so I have not been out walking as much as I should but it will come soon. I am so thankful to be alive and well that I will never take life for granted.

Remembering back to when I was still under anesthesia, I saw a whole bunch of black spiders walking around in my brain and I even asked Nancy what they were doing there. I remember when they stuck the probe in my groin because I winced a little and that is all.

My wife was by my side seeing that I had everything that I needed and making sure that everything was alright. She is the love of my life and my inspiration in everything I do, and I love her.

The very first thing they said was, "Don't become a couch potato." Well, I didn't intend to do that and I could see how easy it would be to fall into that routine. It was easy to follow the exercises they gave me and I have been getting along fine with them. My appetite slowly came back and a good thing because I lost about 15 pounds and was at the weight I was when we got married.

I did have some problems though, when they removed the veins from my legs to use in the bypass surgery. I got an infection. I was told to cover the incision with plastic to avoid infection from the run-off water, but somehow something got in and the hospital had to put special packing in one of the veins and then Nancy had to do the packing at home between visits.

Everyone told me that I would feel better than I did before, which was hard to imagine because I thought I felt pretty good then. The one thing that I must say about all this is that I was not ready to go and leave my beautiful wife in a terrible state. I have a lot of living to do and a few more things to accomplish so my goal is to stay mobile until at least one hundred years old. I intend to keep the promise I made to Nancy; that I will give her more years than I did my first marriage, which lasted 35 years. That's easy; only a few more to go ... and then some.